Catching Up on Conventions

Grammar Lessons for Middle School Writers

Chantal Francois and Elisa Zonana

Foreword by Mary Ehrenworth

HEINEMANN
Portsmouth, NH

To the students of East Side Community High School

Heinemann
361 Hanover Street
Portsmouth, NH 03801–3912
www.heinemann.com

Offices and agents throughout the world

Library of Congress Cataloging-in-Publication Data
Francois, Chantal.
    Catching up on conventions : grammar lessons for middle school writers / Chantal Francois and Elisa Zonana ; foreword by Mary Ehrenworth.
        p. cm.
    Includes bibliographical references.
    ISBN-13: 978-0-325-01282-7
    ISBN-10: 0-325-01282-2
    1. English language—Grammar—Study and teaching (Middle school).   2. English language—Composition and exercises—Study and teaching (Middle school).   I. Zonana, Elisa.   II. Title.

LB1631.F693 2009
428.2071'2—dc22   2008048259

Editor: Kathy Collins
Production: Vicki Kasabian
Cover design: Night & Day Design
Typesetter: Kim Arney
Manufacturing: Louise Richardson

Printed in the United States of America on acid-free paper
13 12 11 10 09 VP 1 2 3 4 5

Contents

Foreword

I n *The Amazing Adventures of Kavalier and Clay*, Michael Chabon tells the story of two boys who long to escape the ordinary confines of their Brooklyn lives. In this process, they dream what he calls "caterpillar dreams," dreams of miraculous escape, release, and transformation. It is the dream of every child who has yearned to become Spiderman or Harry Potter, who is eager to befriend vampires and werewolves, who has wished to fight for Narnia or take the ring to Mordor to the acclaim of Middle Earth. It is a yearning to be different than we are, to live lives of more power, grace, and significance. It is a wish, too, that our tribulations were epic and mythic, in the form of dragons and demons rather than anxiety or lassitude. Those are the real demons of the classroom: apathy, a sense of futility, a fear that it is not worth starting because we cannot accomplish what we wish alone, or that others may not join us, or that we will be misunderstood or mocked or simply ignored by our students or our colleagues. There is nothing, perhaps, more subject to that sense of futility than the teaching of academic English in a rapidly shifting, technological, multilingual, contemporary middle or high school classroom, one where students spend more actual time each day and surely more spontaneous energy mastering the discourses of instant messages, peer expression, and the jargon and norms of television characters than on mastering academic discourse. Yet caterpillar dreams—dreams of change, of personal power, of interdependence, of seemingly miraculous abilities to bridge difference and reimagine identities—are what Chantal and Elisa offer here for the teaching of language. Theirs is a different approach. It is more than grammar instruction. It is something more vital. It is about the potential transformation of the self through language.

There are some explicit aspects of Elisa and Chantal's approach to teaching grammar that make it somewhat different than most others. One is that they work on both sides of the fence that separates workshop methods and drill-and-practice methods. Much of their instruction in grammar is initiated in writing workshop. That is where they get kids to care about their writing and use their increasing control of conventions in meaningful writing endeavors. Yet Chantal and Elisa do provide structures outside of workshop. Most of this skill-drill work aims to help their students learn and practice language codes that are simply different in literary language than they are in the kids' spoken language or the writing they do with and for peers. Chantal and Elisa create lessons for kids because they worry that the everyday work in writing workshop isn't enough to push them beyond language structures that are reinforced every minute kids spend instant messaging or conversing in "teenspeak."

Another way that Chantal and Elisa's instruction may be different is that they themselves visibly act as students of language and pedagogy. Their students know that they read books to learn, that they go to conventions and workshops in order widen their knowledge and deepen their practices. Chantal and Elisa are not interested in setting themselves up as experts, as ones-who-know-the-rules of language. They'll often admit that they find some conventions confusing and that there are some grammar understandings that elude them. It is one reason that they distinguish between errors that an audience may find "glaring and distracting," and conventions that are more literary, that frankly are known and practiced only by a few. It feels important that Chantal and Elisa each model being a person who is always learning. Especially in middle and high school instruction, sometimes it feels as if teachers are uneasy with their mantle of expertise. It is like Superman's cape, it is one that gives us power with parents and colleagues as well as students. It is a dangerous business, though, being an expert, because it makes you vulnerable. It makes new knowledge or fresh methods seem threatening. It means you always have to know everything. It is not intellectually very stimulating. If teaching becomes the act of teaching only what you already know, then your journey is really over. This sense of completion, of already knowing what you want to know, is insidiously infectious. Chantal and Elisa's students work so hard in part because they see their teachers always working on their learning. If the teachers' learning journey were essentially complete, it would be hard to instill a contagious sense of passionate intellectual curiosity in the classroom.

There is one other thing, though, that may make Chantal and Elisa as teachers somewhat different than many of the rest of us, and it is something that I am profoundly moved and humbled by. It is the level of respect and care that they bestow on their students. Undergirding all the work you will see in this book—all the homemade lessons, all the careful bridges constructed between real writing and everyday grammar practice—is an overwhelming sense of urgency. Chantal and Elisa want everything for their students. There is practically nothing that they won't do for them. This matters because it is part of what makes their work in teaching conventions so effective. Their students know that every bit of work they are asked to do, is being asked of them so that they can be more powerful. Chantal and Elisa are completely transparent with their beliefs and desires. They make it clear that teaching literacy is, for them, an act of social justice. When Chantal went to pursue her doctorate at Harvard, and Elisa began studying and teaching at Columbia University's Teachers College, their students knew that they wanted to extend their power to better conditions for more kids in this country. From the first, Elisa and Chantal tell their students that they want them to have access to power, and that academic literacy is part of that access. They tell them honestly that sometimes their language gets in the way of some people understanding them, respecting them, or finding them persuasive. They explain with passion and love that they want their students to be able to speak and write in such a way that they are compelling to many audiences. They never want the kids' language to be something that could hold them back—because they believe that these kids have so much to say that is important. Thus, there is a clarity of purpose, a kind of fearlessness around language codes. Elisa and Chantal are not afraid to say to their students "No, that's not correct," or "Listen to how I'm going to say it and listen hard because it is different than the way you say it."

Elisa and Chantal can be so fierce in the accountability they demand of students because they recognize, respect, and acclaim students' peer, family, and culturally based language patterns. They are not interested in annihilating the kids' natural language. The students know that their teachers value the language they use with their peers—indeed, they'll see their teachers pick up and use some of their language. "Sweet!" and "Snap!" and "I'm gassing you up" can be heard, for instance, in their current conferences. Those words will be different next year, as the kids bring to school a fresh density of creative language. Hence, there is permeability between language codes in their classroom, a dialectic between contemporary expression, and academic codes.

This convergence of language-learning brings us back to the notion that this kind of grammar instruction and practice is embedded in communities that care for one another and in which everyone, adult and child, is always working and learning. That is fierce intellectualism. It is also daunting. Elisa and Chantal know so much about what to teach their kids, because they listen to them outside of the classroom. They study and enjoy their speech patterns in social environments. They teach a reading, writing, and advisory curriculum that embraces the urgent teen social issues that shape the lives of their students. Their school is dedicated to creating a culture of literacy within an atmosphere of transformational possibility. Their colleagues may teach with different methods but there is a universality in their passion for social justice and their belief in their students as young adults with unlimited potential. Chantal and Elisa's grammar instruction, thus, exists within a rich web of curricular and social structures that reinforces students' belief that it is worth it to work hard at academic learning.

The intense beauty of Elisa and Chantal's work can lead to troubling questions, such as: Where then do you begin, if you feel alone in your school? Will you be effective if your work is somewhat isolated in the overall experience your students will have while in your building? What if your kids don't seem to believe that it's worth it to change? What if you despair when wondering where to find time for additional skill work or curricular space for a real writing workshop? What I have learned from Elisa and Chantal is this: *Be courageous*. Start somewhere. Perhaps read through these pages and think first: What of this work am I already almost doing? How could I enhance my current practices so that they extend students' powers more? Then reread and think: What would be next? What will I have to make and do, what conversations with colleagues should I have if I want to add another layer to the work students do and to how I am teaching them?

There are some places where you may have to reconceptualize your curriculum. The most significant rethinking may be about the actual writing tasks students are engaged in. It is impossible to get impassioned writing if the writer has no choice over his or her subject, for instance. Students will not work hard enough at their writing or their language out of obedience to or even affection for their teacher. For students to outgrow themselves as writers they have to care about their writing. To write well, they need to write about subjects which they care deeply about and understand deeply. You may, therefore, need to reconsider whether students ever have opportunities to write about their lives or the teen issues they find most compelling, or the books they love or could love. You may need to ask yourself: Do your students visibly matter in your curriculum? Is the curriculum transparently relevant to the lives they live now and the lives they hope to pursue? Are the students in front of you as important as the curriculum and do they know that?

This question becomes more important in some secondary schools with long-standing traditions of English classes of hard books and scholarly writing tasks. If you take Chantal and Elisa's curricular example, they start the kids in middle school with writing workshop. Their students learn first to write about their own lives, and the books they are reading independently, and the stories they imagine, with increasing power and beauty. They come to understand that writing is a craft and that their teachers will help them get better at it. By high school, the curriculum honors these practices and adds more layers of academic writing to these now more confident and invested writers. The students will have opportunities to write memoir and fiction, and they will do even more persuasive writing, journalism, and literary analysis. You may, therefore, as you embark on the work Elisa and Chantal describe, want to look at the whole curriculum your students experience at your school, and consider what part of a writing curriculum will most benefit your students while they are in your classroom. Ask yourself what writing curriculum will help you teach your students to *care* about learning conventions. If your students are disengaged or disenfranchised, you may want to start with teaching them to write about their own lives. This choice manifestly imbues their lives with significance. As your students master narrative structures and craft, you will also hear their stories, and you can weave mastering conventions into curriculum of empowerment. If your students are essentially engaged, if they believe in their work and your work already, you may wish to emphasize fiction writing and literary analysis, so that you are immersing them in literary language.

Chantal and Elisa demonstrate that it will be to your students' greatest benefit if these decisions are made collegially across a three- or four-year curriculum. If teachers can articulate their writing goals and goals for teaching conventions this way, there is much more chance of the work being transformative. The most important aspect of the work, though, is that it is purposeful. If you can articulate schoolwide purposes and methods in the company of your colleagues, that will be best. If you can articulate departmental and/or grade-level purposes, that's good. If these are beyond your current powers, then articulate your own purposes and methods, and that is still good! You can lean on Chantal and Elisa, they can be your community, as others have been theirs. Teachers such as Alfred Tatum, Lucy Calkins, Don Murray, Donald Graves, bel hooks, Kylene Beers, Nancie Atwell, and so many others—they have all, in their books and their speeches, through the lives they lead and the way they lead us, made us feel less alone in our teaching of language. You'll feel their influence in the pages ahead. I know that Elisa and Chantal too will have an influence. More teachers will say, after considering the work described in the upcoming pages of this book: "I can do this. I can begin work that seems inconceivably hard right now."

It is the great gift that those who go first offer us—they illuminate possibility. They give us a vision. Elisa and Chantal's vision is one of students and teachers working hand-in-hand to increase their powers. It is a vision of classrooms where students are in an apprenticeship position that is not a subservient one, for all that happens in the classroom is for their benefit. Imagine your classroom, its seating arrangements, the books that students will encounter on its shelves, the writing they will see on the walls, the spaces that are designed for them to occupy and to fill with their bodies and their voices. Your grammar instruction will be a part of everything that happens here. Try to get as many books that students would want to read into the room as possible, even if you have to get them from the public library and only one kid at a time can read *Twilight* or *The Pact* or *Tears of a Tiger*. The more they read, the easier it will be to demonstrate and teach them the power of language. Elisa and Chantal's kids have learned to be passionate readers—it is an invisible backdrop to their work. Imagine your ways of being with your students— how you will try to make time and space to pull alongside them as they write and talk, how you will praise and coach them, how you will try to listen to them and model for them. Chantal and Elisa's work happens in all these side-by-side conversations, in the way they show students they care, as well as in the minilessons they give and the work they design for students to get more language practice. When you appropriate their vision, your classroom will become, or will become closer to, a classroom where students learn about writing and how to write, where students are honored for what they know and respected for their potential to know more.

Chantal and Elisa also bestow some clear methods. Implicit in all the teaching of this book is that you would continually assess your students for what they know and are ready to learn next. You may need, therefore, to begin teaching more small groups of students in developmental stages, as you realize that what they know and are ready for is vastly different across your classroom. Elisa and Chantal will show you how to divide up some of this work into all-class work, individual work, and work for particular small groups of students. Or, you may find that the real divergence is between the curriculum and the students, in which case you will need to make insertions into your curriculum so that it meets the literacy and language needs of your actual students. Elisa and Chantal explain the most urgent work that will help your students achieve control over the most immediate conventions of academic language. They will also help you with your explicit instruction, as their own teaching is so tremendously crisp and purposeful. You may choose a different mentor text than they do at times, you may often substitute your own writing example for theirs, but you will be able to copy the teaching point and structure of their lessons. In the same way, you will want to imbue the practice lessons you may make for your students with cultural references to your own community. But you will grasp how to do this when you see how different Chantal and

Elisa's practice lessons are from those of a generic workbook. These practice sessions are quick, purposeful, and part of a spiral curriculum in which students have multiple opportunities to work toward increased mastery.

The boys in Chabon's novel, *The Amazing Adventures of Kavalier and Clay*, transpose their dreams onto the pages of comic books. They imbue their characters with super powers, with miraculous powers of transformation, so that their imagined lives have more power, grace, and heroism than their ordinary ones. These caterpillar dreams of release and transformation are dazzling. Children have loved reading about Harry Potter because he transcends the mundane restraints of his unsatisfactory life. Adolescents have lingered with the vampire Edward, the werewolf Jake, and the human Bella in *Twilight*, in part for these fictional characters' ability to escape the ordinariness and powerlessness of teenage existence. Their endeavors seem grander. Their vision seems longer. Their struggles seem epic and fierce and of significance to others outside themselves. Chantal and Elisa help us imbue the work of the classroom with some of this transformative possibility. There is a gritty realism to their fearless naming of current conditions, and a relentless romanticism to the quest they call their students to take up. It calls on adolescents' urge to be more than they are already. Ultimately, Chantal and Elisa show us the teaching and learning of conventions as part of a personal and collective striving toward proficiency, power, and independence. They help us conceive the daily work of learning language as part of more mythic work, which is that of becoming greater than we were.

Mary Ehrenworth

Preface
Creating a Context That Sustains Powerful Practice

We, Chantal and Elisa, taught at East Side Community High School together for five years before deciding to write about our teaching. We both taught eighth-grade humanities, and we collaboratively planned and then went back to our own classes to teach the curriculum described in this book.

East Side Community High School is located on the Lower East Side of Manhattan. It's a small sixth- through twelfth-grade public school with no selective admissions criteria. Over 80 percent of the students come from low socioeconomic backgrounds. Sixty to 65 percent are Latino (mostly of Puerto Rican and Dominican descent), 30 to 35 percent are African American, and 5 percent are Asian and White. Twenty-eight percent of the students are designated Special Education and 30 percent enter over age, indicating they have been previously held back. While we receive many students who are passionate about writing, most have never had the opportunity to write anything, in or out of school, longer than just a couple of paragraphs.

We share these facts not to define the school or our students, but to provide both the context and setting for our work, and to allow readers to imagine this work in schools with such diverse student population.

The idea to write this book came about after the two of us, as well as other teachers at East Side, named a problem of our practice—that our students struggled with some of the basic rules of Standard Written English. Unfortunately, simply naming the problem didn't help us solve it. We believed that through an ongoing reflective collaboration we could develop instruction to meet our students' needs. We met regularly to look at students' work together so we could identify common areas of struggle. We read and discussed ideas from professional texts about the teaching of grammar, and we attended workshops related to writing and grammar instruction. We held tight to our deeply felt beliefs that students learn best from demonstration teaching and instruction in context, and we challenged ourselves to teach grammar and the conventions of Standard English while also holding on to the integrity of our reading and writing workshops.

In other words, we resisted skill-and-drill, out-of-context, rote-memorization types of grammar exercises, even though resources for those are abundant. We rejected any approaches that didn't show respect for or adequately acknowledge the logic of our students' oral language patterns. Instead, together we developed an approach to teaching grammar and supporting students in using Standard English in both their speaking and writing that is steeped in what we know about best practices for teaching and learning, as well as respectful of our students' backgrounds and modes of discourse. Together, we figured out how to teach grammar within and alongside our reading and writing workshops without losing or diluting their special characteristics. As a result of our collaboration, our professional development, and our profound respect for the identity of our students, we developed a grammar curriculum our students found to be engaging, accessible, and effective.

Acknowledgments

We wouldn't be the teachers and people that we are, and the ideas for this book would never have been, without East Side Community High School. The school's commitments to collaboration, excellent teaching, and opportunities to always get better at what we do encouraged us to take risks and try this grammar curriculum. The staff's belief in, commitment to, and love for the students fiercely challenge the status quo and make East Side a truly special place.

In particular, we would like to thank Mark Federman, principal and leader of a learning community in the truest sense. His tireless, fearless, and passionate commitment to students and staff inspire us all. We would like to thank Kathleen Schechter, our eighth-grade colleague who played an important role in this curriculum's implementation. We would also like to thank the rest of the middle school Humanities team, including Leona Gross, who offered suggestions and support.

Thanks to East Side's class of 2010 for being a part of this curriculum in its early stages, for showing us that this curriculum could be successful, and for challenging us to be better teachers.

Several people played a significant role in the development of this book. Thank you to our editors at Heinemann, Kate Montgomery and Kathy Collins, who saw two fledgling authors through this process. Special thanks to Mary Ehrenworth for believing that our ideas should be shared with a wider audience and to Lucy

Calkins for that small push that made a big difference in our decision to write this book. Thank you also to Theresa Perry for showing enthusiasm for this project and insight on ideas around language, culture, and power in the classroom.

Lastly, we would like to thank our families for believing in us and providing constant support and encouragement.

Introduction

We have to keep asking ourselves, "Is my job to help others accept the unacceptable? Or is it to change the unacceptable?" My own feeling is that it's to change the unacceptable, and that requires both a vision of a better way and abundant moral outrage.

—*Roland Barth, "In Search of Heroes"*

In *Learning by Heart*, Roland Barth (2001) writes, "Perhaps the most powerful asset of the school-based reformer is moral outrage." It is an outrage that so many of our students live in poverty. It is an outrage that so many enter middle school reading and writing far below grade level. It is an outrage that many do not know what an apostrophe is called or how to use one. It is an outrage that schools are an institution of mainstream society that often work, in spite of themselves, to perpetuate inequalities. We ought to be outraged, and it is our job as educators to channel our sense of outrage into reform, both in the classroom and at an institutional level, so that all of our students, no matter their background, home language, or community dialect, have access to the culture of power.

Although many teachers may place great value on both our students' home language and Standard Written English, which we've called *academic language*, the dominant culture in our society does not. By teaching our students Standard English grammatical conventions and how and when and why to code-switch when they speak and write, we are giving our students a key to a world in which they have the right to contribute and participate. After all, knowing how to write and speak in academic language, and knowing how and when to code-switch is integral to attaining equal access. This is undoubtedly political work and it is imperative that we take this on. Providing access to what we consider the culture of power to those without it has been the impetus behind our work together. After all, if we do not provide tools for our students to access the culture of power, then they can neither think critically of it nor reform it. We also believe that it is inherently unfair for those of us who have access to the culture of power to inadvertently deny it to those who don't.

Although we always believed these things, our beliefs weren't always evident in our teaching. In our first few years as teachers of students from high-poverty areas, we both largely avoided teaching grammar. Not because the students didn't need the instruction—they did. Desperately. Not because we didn't care—we did. Deeply. The task just seemed too overwhelming. As soon as we considered instruction on subject–verb agreement we realized that meant students had to know what subjects were, what verbs were, what verb conjugations were, how their own linguistic patterns differed from or matched academic or standard patterns . . . and suddenly the task of teaching subject–verb agreement became a monster. We wondered where in the world to begin, how to teach off of this so it takes hold in our students' lives, and how to fit comprehensive grammar instruction into an already stretched-thin language arts curriculum.

The truth is that grammar and spelling errors were so rampant in our students' writing, and this caught us off guard. Like many of our colleagues, when we started teaching middle school, we didn't think we'd be faced with students who needed intensive and comprehensive grammar instruction. If we ever imagined teaching grammar, we envisioned teaching the occasional grammar lesson, as the need arose. As writing workshop teachers who believed in the power of giving our students time every day in class to read and write in meaningful ways, we held the unspoken hope that students who read often and wrote often would somehow absorb correct usage. After all, if our students were engaged in reading and writing workshop, reading books of their choice for thirty to ninety minutes a day, and writing in multiple genres on topics of their choice throughout the year, wouldn't they inadvertently learn grammar and spelling? Unfortunately, this learning by osmosis wasn't happening automatically for many of our students, and consequently, their grammar and spelling errors interfered with their proficiency as writers and their ability to communicate their powerful ideas.

Yet, this is not a problem particular only to our students in our middle and high school classrooms. In fact, students' weak grasp of grammar conventions is an urgent issue in college readiness. Researchers find that at least 30 percent to 40 percent of incoming college freshmen require college remediation courses that support their weak mastery of writing conventions (Attewell, Lavin, Domina, and Levey 2006). Additionally, researchers disagree on these programs' effectiveness in supporting students toward college graduation (Martorell and McFarlin 2007). Regardless of their effectiveness, students often spend their first year in college paying full tuition for remediation classes that earn them no college credit. For students from low-income families, this is just one more factor that makes it difficult for them to persist toward graduation (Chajet 2006).

We knew that our students needed direct, explicit, wise instruction and it was our job to figure out how to give them that. We needed to find a way to equip them with mastery of the English language, which in turn would lead them to have greater cultural and social capital. It's undeniable that people are judged on the way they speak and write, and they are judged even more so when they are African American, Latino, and living in high poverty, like most of our students.

We understand that our students come to us with their own valid and logical patterns of communication, and through our teaching of grammar we emphasize the importance of being able to code-switch. In other words, instead of teaching our students that the way they talk or write is wrong or bad, we teach our students to consider the audience and the message they are trying to communicate and to be accountable to the rules of grammar, especially in academic and formal writing.

After all, grammar and spelling errors are highly visible and often the first thing that a reader notices. We were trained to look beyond the errors in order to focus on and appreciate the content, voice, and process of their writing. Therefore, much of our instruction focused on teaching students how to generate ideas, develop content, and follow a process beginning with drafting and ending with publishing their writing for real audience. We were, and are still committed to this approach to teaching writing. But we recognized that not directly or explicitly addressing their grammar and spelling needs was doing a disservice to our students. We knew that even if we could look beyond their errors, the world outside of our classroom wouldn't. Mainstream society judges young adults of color from low-income backgrounds, by their skin color, their clothing choices, and the way they talk. Society also judges them by the way they write and their ability to use Standard English grammar and spelling conventions. We couldn't deny that knowing and using the rules of Standard English grammar would give our students a form of capital that will help them access college, gainful employment, and positions of power so that they may can work to dismantle various societal boundaries.

Realizing all this was one thing, but figuring out how to teach to affect profound change presented another challenge altogether.

This book shares the process and product of our work as we developed a grammar curriculum that made a difference for our students. We view our approach to grammar instruction as both an enrichment to the writing and reading workshop and a departure from the traditional, out-of-context, skill-and-drill grammar instruction. When we implemented this curriculum, our own expectations for what we believed our students could do in their writing were raised. The power in our students' narrative and expository writing was strengthened by their keen attention to conventions in academic English. Our students navigated the writing process with clear objectives and intentions. When they edited, they had new, concrete tools. In their reflections about learning to use Standard English conventions in their writing, many students commented that they felt they were becoming better writers who were more ready for the whole world to see their writing and take it seriously.

We have divided our book into two sections. In Part 1, we provide an overview of the curriculum and suggestions for how to implement it. We share ideas about ways to listen to students' oral language and look at students' writing in order to make instructional plans that are based on students' strengths and needs. The chapters in Part 2 offer suggestions for instruction about different topics in the grammar curriculum, such as lessons to move students away from *inaudible* errors (apostrophe use, for example), as well as *audible* errors (such as subject–verb agreement and code-switching) in academic language. We also supply lessons to support students in code-switching. Finally, we offer ideas for reinforcement and holding students accountable to what they've learned, suggestions for meaningful assessment, and we show examples of students' work and evidence of their progress.

Through our collaboration to develop an effective grammar curriculum, the two of us became better teachers and our students became better able to make informed decisions in their writing. We hope you think of this book as a guide to the content and methods to teach grammar that we've found successful in our own classrooms.

PART

1

First Steps

1

Rethinking Grammar

Building the Foundation for Instruction

In the spring of 2004, after our students submitted the final drafts of their business letters, we contemplated different ways that they could share their work. Students had already sent their letters off to local politicians, authors, and company executives, but we wanted our students to have an even bigger audience because the letters were exemplars of students' ability to find voice, meaning, and passion through writing.

Students had thought carefully and deeply about topics that mattered to them, like universal health insurance, the preservation of local parks, and safety in schools. They had searched online and in the news for the most recent information related to the problems they identified and strategized about to whom they should address their letters. At the end of the unit, they felt like they had contributed their voice to current debates on important topics. We were ready to share their success with their families.

We sent a letter home with students asking that the adults read students' letters and comment on their strengths and weaknesses. We were eager to hear what parents thought about our students' writing, and as soon as we collected the sheets that morning in class, we flipped through parents' responses. Unexpectedly, the same feedback appeared over and over: "Why are there so many spelling errors?" and "The writing mistakes confused me," or "She should have done a better job correcting her grammar."

We were taken aback that the one thing that we had deemphasized in promoting writing workshop was the very thing that our students' families wanted to bring to our attention. Their families' comments sent a powerful and unambiguous message. They wanted to know, how did we let our students complete pieces of writing, and in fact send them out to the world, without holding them accountable to the standards of written academic English? The families' concerns caused us to question our belief that at times it's enough to celebrate our students' deeply felt sense of purpose and their attention to craft when they write.

This experience brought to mind Lisa Delpit's (1995) assertion that in schools, when those who are in the culture of power are not explicit about the rules of that culture, they ultimately keep power out of reach from those who do not possess it. Thus, while many mainstream educators who do not acknowledge their informal assumptions about race, class, and power in the classroom are well meaning, their progressive, liberal efforts ultimately contribute to inequality in our society. This happens even though parents want something more. Delpit (1995) writes, "Parents who are outside of this culture of power want to ensure that the school provides their children with discourse patterns, interactional styles, and spoken and written language codes that will allow them success in larger society" (88). In our classroom, despite our intentions, we failed to meet our students' and families' expectations of helping students gain access to worlds outside of their own.

Experiences such as these became catalysts for developing a sense of urgency in thinking about how to join issues of power and access with the rules of academic language in our writing curriculum. When we began to collaborate on our grammar curriculum, we realized that we shared three main concerns:

1. How could we fit in grammar instruction without compromising the integrity of our writing workshop or forcing aside other parts of our curriculum?

2. How could we create a grammar curriculum that would capitalize on what we know about best teaching practices?

3. How could we support students' code-switching between everyday language and academic language, despite the injustice of language and power in our society?

Fitting in More Grammar Instruction Without Compromising the Writing Workshop

Because our students developed into powerful writers on many levels during writing workshop, we did not want to compromise on the time spent writing. We also knew they needed more comprehensive instruction on grammar. Unsurprisingly, we felt wary about devoting too much focused time on grammar instruction at the expense of writing workshop.

Using what we knew about the workshop from educators like Nancie Atwell, Lucy Calkins, Ralph Fletcher, Carl Anderson, and Laura Robb, our writing workshop offered writing for real purposes and to real audiences, something we knew was crucial, not only to our students' growth as writers but to applications of grammar as well. However, we were only able to fold in one or two grammar lessons during each unit of study, as teaching the strategies for writing within particular genres took concentrated amounts of time. Our students needed more instruction than this. We also felt that we didn't have the time in our middle school classrooms to approach grammar through inquiry and immersion. That, too, would compromise the workshop structures we felt committed to maintaining. Again, Delpit's (1995) words echo this quandary: "Unless one has the leisure of a lifetime of immersion to learn them, explicit presentation makes learning immeasurably easier" (228).

When we started teaching writing through the structure of writing workshop to our middle school students, our vision was centered around teaching skills and strategies for writing via a particular genre. Beyond just wanting students to learn how to write an essay that followed the structure and organization of the genre, we were committed to working with students to develop writing that mattered and that helped them effectively communicate who they were to the world.

Our unit and daily lesson plans included strategies to teach students how to identify and write powerfully about topics that they cared about as adolescents thereby asserting their identities in the world. We included genres such as editorials, business letters, poetry, and narratives because we knew that these forms of writing would provide students a vehicle to communicate their reflections, desires, and personal experiences in poignant ways. As Nancie Atwell (2002) suggests, this perspective on teaching writing helps students answer the question, "so what?" In encouraging our students to write about what mattered to them, they found the meaning in their written words and ultimately found meaning in the purpose of writing.

Our professional development enabled us to develop a sequence of units in teaching that followed a similar trajectory:

- Students immerse themselves in a given genre by reading models by student and adult authors to understand the features of structure, tone, and organization.
- They learn how to identify topics they deemed worth writing about and write freely on those topics.

- Students practice the specific traits of that genre (e.g., learning the structure of a body paragraph in an editorial).
- After practicing the basic components of the genre, students draft their own pieces.
- Students engage in writing partnerships throughout the process to hear and provide feedback on content and structure.
- They learn ways to revise their piece (e.g., learning how to add details to a particular scene in an anecdote).
- After revising, students reread their work to check for errors in spelling and basic conventions.
- When students complete and turn in their final drafts, they celebrate their peers' pieces by reading and providing feedback to each other.

The sequence of our writing workshop units created a space for producing provocative writing in which students relayed their fearful, triumphant, angry, and amusing life experiences. We remember a student's gripping anecdote about the day her brother returned from deployment in Iraq. Another student wrote a business letter to her landlord complaining about overdue apartment repairs (and received a prompt response!). Yet another student wrote an editorial proposing solutions to the kinds of bullying middle school students face every day. We read dozens of poems on heartbreak and friendship, learned about the threats of homophobia, and fell in love with our students again and again when they invited us into their life-defining moments. Our students submit about fifteen to twenty final drafts of writing to us each year, and each piece is an assertion of their risk taking, identity, and growth.

We didn't want to lose any of this. We simply did not want it to encroach on the time it took for our students to develop into strong writers, and we only folded in one or two lessons on conventions during each unit of study. These lessons would tend to occur while students were in their editing stages, when we first introduced some basic steps of editing. For example, we applied Nancie Atwell's (2002) and Laura Robb's (2004) suggestion that students whisper their drafts aloud and use a colored pencil to make changes to make the act of editing visible and audible. The editing stage was also a time for us to make quick, sweeping suggestions: "Remember to add end punctuation!" or "Use the dictionary for spelling!" While these recommendations could be useful, the way we introduced them to the class, with little context or meaning, rendered them temporary solutions to ongoing problems. Our students needed more instruction than this.

We decided we needed to fold in small, fifteen-minute chunks of time three days a week to provide grammar instruction.

Designing Grammar Instruction That Incorporates Best Teaching Practices

Instead of allowing work on conventions to interfere with writing workshop, we tried to introduce formal grammar lessons. We pored over instructional grammar texts but struggled to find one that specifically addressed our students' most urgent writing needs. Many workbooks differentiated among a dozen different kinds of verbs and asked students to diagram decontextualized, meaningless sentences. Instead of finding a text that could help students make informed choices about effective communication, we only found ones that purported to be objective authorities on the English language. Still, we settled on a workbook and introduced its forty-minute lessons into our Humanities blocks. Our students' grumbling was not as surprising as its lack of transfer to writing workshop—we observed virtually none. While students whizzed through fill-in-the-blanks worksheets and circled the correct number of nouns in a sentence, when the opportunity came for students to apply what they learned to their drafts and freewrites in writing workshop, we saw little evidence that they had internalized what we taught.

We found that traditional grammar lessons designed for middle school students were generally too comprehensive for some of the basic elements our students grappled with. It seemed that the available texts didn't address the diversity of middle school writers and how students' multiple cultural identities inform their use of the English language. While we struggled to find the best approach for teaching grammar, we knew we had to create a method of grammar instruction that would address and accomplish several things in order to be successful.

The method had to:

- *Address only one aspect of grammar at a time.* We borrowed this feature from our experiences with teaching reading and writing minilessons. In the *Art of Teaching Writing,* Lucy Calkins (1994) suggests that minilessons that focus on a single writing strategy can be powerful opportunities for students to digest just a small nugget of information at a time. This notion translates beautifully to our needs in a grammar curriculum, whereby we can provide students with one small piece of knowledge about conventions that they can embrace at a given moment instead of overwhelming them with numerous features of language all at once.
- *Be designed so that each new lesson or unit built on the ones that came before.* Our curriculum planning has also enabled us to value a cumulative learning experience as opposed to decontextualized lessons in a random sequence.

Our ideal grammar curriculum would allow students to see how different features of written language relate to one another in a seamless and organized way.

- *Ensure transfer by providing opportunities to use what they learn in real academic contexts.* Our prior experience with grammar instruction that was unrelated to authentic writing was unsuccessful. Students proved that they could master conventions on a worksheet but when it came to real writing experiences, we could not find evidence of what they practiced during a grammar lesson that had occurred just twenty minutes prior! We knew that students needed an immediate opportunity to edit or draft sentences in order to transfer what they had just learned to a genuine writing experience. We also knew that we needed to make our classroom environments reflect the grammar work by building in multiple extensions and making the work visible in multiple contexts. As teachers, we had to take this work on with fervor, and our classrooms had to be evidence of our efforts.

- *Provide ongoing practice and accountability of rules learned.* To increase the degree of transfer, we planned to include standard English rules that students acquired in the formative and summative assessments of all writing experiences in Humanities. Thus, we would measure students' growth in each area of grammar directly on their writing workshop rubrics.

- *Be short so as not to lose or bore students and fit easily into an already busy curriculum.* We wanted our grammar instruction to be a vehicle for students to become more powerful readers, writers, and historians. Therefore, we wanted to design a program that would complement, and not encroach upon, what students were already learning during independent reading, reading workshop, writing workshop, and social studies.

- *Be accessible in student-friendly language.* We wanted the text of the curriculum to include enough familiar background knowledge to avoid the extra work of decoding and comprehending unfamiliar text. While we value this work, staying faithful to a short and deliberate lesson focused on conventions was an important priority. We knew that we could support students' access to texts during other parts of the Humanities block.

- *Directly address our students' patterns of language (ones that come from their oral language patterns, or ones that are significant in written language but not in oral language).* We wanted to design a grammar instruction curriculum that would simultaneously meet students where they were and also expose them to new ways of writing English. We knew that we could achieve this only if we listened well to what they said and focused closely on how they wrote.

These practices would enable us to design a curriculum reflective of who our students were, instead of a commercial grammar curriculum that would not necessarily consider our students' identity to the degree that we could.

Supporting Students' Code-Switching Between Everyday and Academic Language

At a basic level, *code-switching* describes the conscious act of alternating between different languages and knowing when, how, and why to do it. Code-switching may involve more than just language; it can include tone and style of speech, gestures, dress, and essentially entire ways of being. It follows, then, that code-switching happens in both oral and written contexts, but oral code-switching might allow for an easier transition from one language or dialect to the next than doing it on paper. In this curriculum, we aim to address the *written* aspects of code-switching. Geneva Smitherman, a sociolinguist and education activist, has written that students' ability to code-switch "is a behavioral manifestation of the interaction of race and class" (2000, 143). That is, when people code-switch, they cross barriers of race in class through the way they speak and write. When students do not possess this skill, they may experience language barriers in school and in other mainstream settings.

Thus, Smitherman (2000) asserts that the issue of code-switching is beyond whether students should learn Standard English. Instead, she suggests that educators need to appropriately frame the context under which it is taught. She posits, "righteous teachers taking care of business in the English classroom must see to it that kids learn to compose coherent, documented, specific, logical—in short, rhetorically powerful oral and/or written communications" (348–49). She urges practitioners to focus on the nuances of grammar conventions as well as the instruction of effective discourse styles in various settings. Smitherman's argument suggests that knowledge of subject–verb agreement in academic language can only take a writer so far, and not far enough, if the writer hasn't found sufficient evidence to support his or her viewpoint in an essay. Indeed, we would like to think that our curriculum is in some ways a means to the end of our students achieving a sophisticated, complex, writing voice.

Our attitude is that our students' voices, no matter how similar to or different from our own, ought to be valued and appreciated in our classrooms, in their homes and neighborhoods, and in larger society. Unfortunately, there are those individuals, many of whom are gatekeepers to high school and college admissions, as well as those in decision-making positions in the workforce, who do not agree. As we celebrate our students for who they are, we also recognize that we live in a society that can be quick to prejudge and discriminate because of appearance and discourse. Our charge, therefore, is to prepare our students for that society, however unjust it may be, because ignoring the intersections between language and power only perpetuates the inequality that exists. At the same time, we hope that through this curriculum, our students become powerful purveyors of communication who can stand up to a society that favors assimilation to one English and views speakers of other English languages and dialects as anything other than legitimate.

When students approach and enter adolescence, they need more justifications for what they are learning than they perhaps did when they were younger. Instruction for middle school students needs to be different, we believe, than for students in earlier grades. Mary Ehrenworth and Vicky Vinton, authors of *The Power of Grammar* (2004), are correct when they say that showing students how grammar affects meaning in their writing is a way to encourage them to make grammatical decisions they might have ignored otherwise. That is true for the artful decisions: where to put the period, whether to use a semicolon or a comma. Students should know and use these rules effectively so they can make themselves understood in their writing as clearly as possible. We wouldn't want to lose this aspect of the teaching of grammar. However, for some grammatical errors, art does not enter into the discussion. How and when to use apostrophes, for instance, or how to spell homophones or plural nouns, depend more on hard-and-fast rules—and can be extraordinarily distracting to a reader when used incorrectly. In order to address these distracting errors, students need a different motivation. Simply saying something is correct or incorrect is not enough for them to break habits and learn new ways of writing. Students need a reason to do so, one that goes beyond grades or saying that something is wrong. And the reason is this: The world beyond the classroom, though unfair at times, is the place where they will gain access to academic and professional settings through writing with academic language.

Because we want our students to have access to that power, we want them to be equipped with all the tools that will make that access possible. Being explicit with students about this can feel tricky, but we believe it is essential. We think introducing the grammar work with all this in mind helps to maximize student buy-in early on. Here is how an introduction to students could sound:

> We are going to be focusing more on grammar and spelling. In telling you why, I'm going to say some things that that I know to be true, and that you may know to be true as well. As your teacher, I want certain things for you. I want

you to love reading and writing, and I want you to get better and better at it. I also want other people to recognize each of you for your talents, to read something you have written and to think, "Wow. This is someone to take seriously." I can see that you have important experiences and ideas to share with the world. However, we do not live in a fair world. People are sometimes judged because of the color of their skin or because of where they live or how much money they have. This is prejudice. People are also judged on their writing. When people see writing that is full of errors, they are distracted and unable to see anything beyond those errors. As students of color, this is something you cannot afford. In learning certain rules around grammar in academic language and making that knowledge your habit, your words and voices will be heard more loudly, more clearly, because you are not allowing errors in academic language to give people permission to ignore or discriminate against you. This is essential to your access to many of the privileges, comforts, and necessities in life. You deserve those things, and learning this will help you to have access to them. In fact, by gaining access to these rules, we hope that you will pursue the power to help people rethink the way some people judge others in our society simply because of the way they talk or write.

We believe as students change from childhood to adolescence, from elementary to middle school, an approach to learning must address the real-world application—the answer to the question "How will this affect my life right now?" Correct usage of conventions in Standard English fits right in, and explicitly sharing that with students is an important aspect of this curriculum.

In these honest conversations with students, notice how we talk about the importance of our students' Standard English rule acquisition. We tell them that understanding these rules provides access and capital in mainstream life that they currently do not have. It is also important that we stress that this is not how we would like the world to be, but that acquiring the rules of Standard English gives our students the power necessary to question and reform the very structures that value mainstream language over nonmainstream languages.

Indeed, we want students to understand why their knowledge of code-switching is a crucial skill that prepares them for mainstream society while allowing them to question the mainstream cultural beliefs. It is important that we communicate to our students why there is a need to study the conventions of Standard English. We want to discuss with them that dominant society dictates who gets listened to and how people listen to them. We need to share with them that these factors are very much related to the type of language they use as well as their particular audience. Indeed, in this society, the way that we write says a lot about how much and what kind of power our voices command (Bourdieu 1991). It is also important for us to hold these conversations in ways that did not denigrate who they are, but instead prepare them to make informed choices about the type of language they use in all the different settings they encounter.

The term *code-switching* implies a going back and forth, switching from one code (or language pattern) to another. While much of what our students wrote in school demanded academic language, we would have been both mistaken and doing a disservice if we didn't explicitly explore when and where everyday language is more appropriate than academic language.

First, students must consider their audience and voice when code-switching. When writing essays, business or political letters, or responses on tests, students need to know that these more formal genres require academic language. Second, we encourage academic language in our classrooms, such as in class discussions, since the classroom is an academic setting. However, there are other forms of writing and talk in which everyday language is more appropriate. We explored how fiction, personal narrative, and poetry are all genres in which authors often make choices to use everyday language for effect. We considered the poetry and fiction of Langston Hughes, the dialogue in much of Walter Dean Myers' writing or Lorraine Hansberry's *A Raisin in the Sun*, to name a few. We studied *The Skin I'm In*, in which Sharon G. Flake writes entirely in everyday language, including the narration. All of these authors use everyday language to make their writing sound authentic, giving genuine voice to characters, and bringing setting alive with truth and accuracy. It is the conscious decision making on the part of the writer that must be clear to the reader: Despite the injustice of it, many readers will view writing in everyday language negatively unless it is an obvious, stylistic choice made by the author.

Once we considered our major ideas about designing a grammar curriculum, we then turned our attention to identifying students' needs.

2

Looking at Student Writing and Listening to Student Talk to Inform Instruction

"We don't got no homework," Imen, an eighth-grade student in Elisa's class, declared one morning.

Aside from the fact that they did indeed have homework, Elisa first wanted to help Imen with her grammar.

"We don't *got no* homework, or we don't *have any* homework?" Elisa asked her, assuming Imen would rephrase her statement in "correct" English.

"We don't got no homework," she answered.

"Wait," Elisa persisted. "Which one sounds right: we don't *got no* homework or we don't *have any* homework?"

"*We don't got no homework* sounds right," Imen said.

Several other students nodded in agreement. *Sounds right.* Of course, the double negative sounded right to Imen. It *was* right. It was not right according to the codes of standard, academic English, but it was right according to the codes of many of our students' home and cultural languages. Elisa's loaded blunder made her realize there was no *right* answer; there were only different patterns of speech and choices about which pattern to use in different contexts. And, while it may be unfair, Elisa knew that Imen and the other students would need to understand and choose codes depending on where they were, who they were talking to, or what they were hoping to accomplish. It was an "a-ha" moment for Elisa and it forced her into a larger understanding of language and of her responsibilities as an educator.

The incident with Imen was a reminder that language and culture are deeply connected, and that as teachers, we are responsible for understanding that. James Gee (2001) teaches us that language is situated in a sociocultural context. That is, we do not use words simply to string words together, but instead our experiences in the world—both at home and at school—influence how we use language. He writes, "language is not about conveying neutral or objective information; rather, it is about communicating perspectives on experience and action in the world, often in contrast to alternative and competing perspectives" (Gee 2001, 716). Gee's theories hold important implications for how we approached this curriculum. Here, we aimed for our students' new knowledge in writing academic English to complement what they already knew about words and the world, beyond just working with them in a closed system of meaningless symbols and spelling patterns. To achieve this goal would require us to have a better sense of how our students use language to make sense of the world. Two of the most authentic ways to discover what our students know, believe, and need to learn about written and oral language is to listen to their talk and to look at their writing in a variety of contexts.

Listening Closely to Students' Oral Language to Help Inform Grammar Instruction

We consider listening to be an important form of doing the research necessary to inform these lessons. Once we acknowledged the connection between what our students said and what we saw in their writing, we began to pay closer attention to the phrases and sentences our students used when they spoke to us and each other. Instead of consulting a text that would predict what we might hear our students say, we let our own students' words be the data for our upcoming lesson plans. This was essential as it kept the work both current and relevant. We listened everywhere—in the cafeteria, in the hallway, and in our classes—to better understand the ways our students crafted what they said. We filled the margins and corners of our notebooks with these excerpts whenever we could steal a moment during or between classes. Then, we would share these findings, along with those from students' raw writing samples, discuss what we were learning about our students here, and then determine the ways in which our findings would help us design our next lessons.

Before approaching a new understanding of the way our students make sense of language in their writing, we identified with those teachers who considered themselves, as Wheeler and Swords (2006) call them, "correctionists." This model "diagnoses (or rather, misdiagnoses) the child's home speech as 'poor English' or 'bad grammar,' finding that the child 'does not know how to show plurality, possession, and tense,' or the child 'has problems' with these" (31). Again, the correctionist perspective holds that there is a right way to produce language, and this jointly implies that any other way is deficient or wrong. In the classroom, our correctionist actions led us to arm ourselves with pens and colored pencils, ready to eradicate and change what our students had written in the hopes that ultimately the student would acquire the right way. And in our planning meetings, our correctionist talk sounded like, "What are we going to do to fix all the errors we see in their writing?" These beliefs, actions, and conversations stemmed from our understanding of the power of academic language in our own writing education and reflected the mainstream view that there is one right way to write and speak English.

Wheeler and Swords (2006) push teachers to let go of their traditional assumptions of how language ought to be constructed, which suggests that many students are doing things the wrong way in the form of errors. They advise that teachers look at students' writing and start to describe what is there—what patterns, forms, and codes students enact in their writing, what structures they adopt, and what features of their own work they can use to begin thinking of other ways of communicating in the classroom. What teachers might see, then, is that students are not all wrong all the time just because their spelling and verb forms are different than that of Standard English. Moreover, teachers may also see that students use patterns in their writing that mirror the way they speak. Finally, teachers will see that the way students make sense of writing is not only a reflection of their skin color or class but a connection to the universal issues surrounding understanding the difference between oral and written communication.

Studying the students' actual speech helped us to better navigate this territory. Take a look at a few common sentences we heard from our students:

- "We don't got no homework."
- "That don't make no sense."
- "I been told you that."
- "That's mines."

A chart of patterns and teaching implications would look something like this:

Everyday Language Patterns	Implications for Teaching
"We don't got not homework"; "That don't make no sense."	Double negatives; subject–verb agreement; *got* vs. *have*
"I been told you that."	*Been* vs. *already*
"That's mines."	*Mine* as singular

Many of these patterns make their way into the students' writing. Taking a look at a raw written excerpt from one of Roxanne's writer's notebook entries can help to illustrate this point. Roxanne, an eighth-grade student, wrote this entry early in September.

> As me and my best friend genisis was going to 8st and Avenue D to see my friend nana. Genisis was wearing this short tube top that showed her belly button pearsing. As we was near the park we saw nana, Harold and his cousins. As I saw Harold I was thinking to myself "Oh no", why Harold got to be here. I already knew a fight was about to happen between genisis and Harold cause I could feel it through my skin. See Harold never keeps his mouth closed, he's a small boy with a lot of things to say, and his girl was there so everyone knew he was going to make a show. So when we got there we started talking to nana and been telling her whats been going on this week. I told nana that I wanted to get my belly button pearsed. So how Harold had heard because hes was overhearing our conversation.

So, what do we observe the student doing? She is

- Using speech patterns in writing:
  - (subject–verb agreement patterns) "me and my best friend genisis was going"; "As we was near the park"
  - "why Harold got to be here"
  - "been telling her"
  - "cause"

- Using proper nouns:
  - Avenue D
  - Genisis
  - Harold

- Following a sentence structure

- Using beginning and ending punctuation
- Using punctuation for dialogue

This is an important place to begin because many of Roxanne's "errors" in fact mirror her speech patterns. Studying both home or "everyday" language patterns and "academic" or "Standard Written English" patterns and making the idea of code-switching explicit is the way to approach errors like the ones Roxanne is making in her notebook. Despite the injustice of it, readers are likely to assume that writing like this is filled with errors unless the writer is making clear choices to include parts in everyday language. Specifically, since this is a narrative, Roxanne could choose to keep some of the writing in everyday language and change some to academic language to accentuate voice. For example, when she shares her inner thoughts and writes, "why Harold got to be here," she could decide to write this just as it is, in everyday language, to accurately depict her thoughts in writing. Unless that is a conscious choice she makes (revealed perhaps by using everyday language for dialogue and inner thinking, and academic language for narration), it will appear to the reader as an error, however unjust that assumption is.

Listening to our students speak and studying their speech patterns allowed us to see some the "errors" in their writing for what they actually were: reflections of their spoken spelling and verb forms. This gave us an entry point for teaching. The teaching became not about fixing errors but about code-switching.

Learning from Students' Writing

Reviewing student writing with colleagues is invaluable: it impacts teaching, learning, interrater reliability, collegiality, and professionalism. Looking at student writing is a truly authentic form of data collection. It gives you insight into what the students are doing, with what they are struggling, and who the students are. It is the best resource material from which to design a grammar curriculum—and the material is at your fingertips. It allows you to direct your teaching in pointed and meaningful ways, and it ensures that the focus is on what the students are doing and learning and not just on what lessons have been taught.

For all units in writing workshop, we have students follow the writing cycle: collecting, planning, drafting, revising, editing, and publishing. While it is important to examine what students are doing with grammar and spelling throughout the writing cycle (and students are assessed for what they can do in different stages), looking at raw or on-demand student writing is the most authentic writing for determining what grammar and spelling issues the students are having because it shows what they are doing habitually and automatically.

Using Raw Writing as Data

By *raw* writing we mean writing that has not been touched by the teacher's hands or words. It is writing that the student produces independently, revealing the student's independent and habitual practices. Lucy Calkins (1994) suggests beginning each year asking the students to write a story "on demand"—in one sitting with no instruction. The easiest places to find raw writing are in students' writer's notebooks and in on-demand writing.

Had we assessed our students solely with generic multiple-choice or fill-in-the-blank grammar quizzes, we would have left ourselves bereft of an opportunity to have a keener sense of who our students are, what drives their passions, how they understand the world, and how they use conventions habitually and automatically in actual writing to communicate their understandings. These kinds of assessments are based on a perspective that there is only one right way to write, and this way often reflects a dominant ideology in this society. Thus, such assessments perpetuate and promote the identity of mainstream culture while simultaneously denigrating others. Furthermore, such assessments treat conventions and the features of academic language as isolated aspects of writing rather than understanding how students construct language. By using raw writing, we encourage students to establish their voice by building on what they know instead of starting a unit by showing them all that they may not know.

Our use of raw and on-demand student writing is the one way that allows us to better understand our students' specific strengths and weaknesses in writing. We can identify the explicit features of writing that will help our students become more powerful, fluent writers in the discourse of dominant, mainstream culture. Using students' raw and on-demand writing first, therefore, brings us closer to a pedagogical goal of preparing students to learn how to read the world and learn how to transform it. Ultimately, examining our students' work as a first step in this process is critical to its success.

While any raw writing will suffice for looking for students' habits and independence levels—writer's notebook entries, for example—we think the on-demand pieces are especially valuable for assessment.

We emphasize the significance of relating this work to writing workshop because it is in this context that students establish their own voice and learn what it means to represent the way they see the world through their own words. Therefore, looking at students' raw on-demand writing is a powerful, reflective endeavor for us as we learn more about who our students are through their writing (without the constraints of teacher directives) and how they make sense of the world, language, and words. When our students produce such personal writing, we find many leads to steps we can take in later units and lessons in writing workshop: how our students conceive of personal and social issues, anecdotes of life experiences, as well as the technical attributes of their writing.

Assessing Growth in On-Demand Writing Pieces

The on-demand writing idea became central to our grammar and writing curricula. Before and after each unit, we would ask the students to write an on-demand piece in the genre we were studying. Examining the on-demand piece *before teaching* a unit allowed us to get a sense of students' current writing strengths and weaknesses and informed what lessons we would teach. Examining the on-demand piece *after publishing* allowed us—and the students—to see their growth. This practice provided valuable data that informed our instruction and gave us a real benchmark for assessment. Asking students to do the same by looking at their writing before and after having gone through the writing cycle and publishing essays provided data that allowed us to assess individual progress as well as general progress in grammar and spelling (as well as in other areas). Comparing the two on-demand written pieces, and comparing the two to their published pieces, allows for truly authentic summative assessment that shows what the students can do, and when they can do it. We decided to include the second on-demand piece in their grade for that writing unit. It didn't seem logical or fair to count that first sample because it was a measure of where they were *before* instruction. The second piece, however, seems to be a measurement of both their growth and their abilities because they demonstrate what they can do independently as a result of practicing strategies and skills in a given genre. This final on-demand piece is a more accurate representation of a student's writing growth than a published piece that goes through multiple reviewers and teacher input. We grade the second on-demand piece against the same rubric we use for their published pieces but we omit the elements of process or habits. It is only achievement that we are looking at here. (Grading, rubrics, and assessment pieces are discussed further in Chapter 6.)

One convenient aspect of these on-demand assessments is that they work for any unit of writing you may be teaching: narrative, essay, short story, play, poetry, business or political letter. It is a nice way to bookend each unit of study; each unit begins and ends with an on-demand writing sample. In only adding these two writing periods to each unit throughout the year, you are gaining invaluable data that serves to inform instruction and as a tool for real assessment.

Developing Implications for Grammar Instruction by Examining Student Writing

The better you become at examining your students' writing, the more adept you will be at understanding who they are as writers and what their strengths and weaknesses are in terms of Standard Written English. It is important to look not just with the lens of what students could *not* do, but with the lens of how they are making sense of language. After a broader look, we look at our students' writing specifically in order to determine what grammar and spelling rules we need to teach. In fact, it was reading their writing that forced us to acknowledge that we had to teach more grammar and spelling rules than we had been making time for in our curriculum. This knowledge will help you address questions around pacing a grammar curriculum, such as: What are the areas that you think address your students' most immediate needs? Do they need more or less frequent practice during the week? Which area of grammar will build on the next areas that you have identified? As you begin to ponder these questions, your answers may be similar to the ones that we have, and your curriculum might look a lot like ours. It is possible, however, that your students may have different qualities of writing and therefore may need different support. Making those decisions about your students demonstrates the authenticity of this curriculum: It is intended to specifically address the needs of your student writers.

Another argument for looking at student work is that it is an opportunity to look at and learn about students as whole people. We can think about their identity, who they are, and what matters to them. As our students represent a range of cultural and ethnic backgrounds, it was important to caution ourselves from making sweeping generalizations about the relationship between their writing and their identity. For example, some of our African American students possess speech patterns that are different than our Latino students and our Asian American students. Still, identifying our students by these ethnic categories is hardly sufficient in understanding the complexity of our students' language and writing issues. Indeed, not all of our Latino students, for example, speak and write in the same way. Furthermore, class and geography also play a role in their speech patterns. It is important to keep some of this in mind when looking at student work, while remembering that generalizations can be risky. Grounding these ideas in student writing helps to keep this work accurate. In that way, we were able to notice patterns that informed our teaching in crucial ways. We noticed that lessons needed to teach rules specific only to writing—like apostrophe use and the spelling of homophones. Other lessons needed to be around code-switching, as students often used oral language patterns, like double negatives, in both their spoken and written language. Studying our students' writing enabled us to make a plan for teaching, whereby we identified universal areas of difficulty in academic writing and created a sequence of instruction. To get a sense of what this work can look like, take a look at a typical sample of student writing that follows and the areas for instruction that developed from it.

William's Writer's Notebook Entry

The first day I went to a Pet shop. I was only 7. In my mom's eye's, thats old enough to have a pet. So I walk in. this huge guy comes up to me and say:
"hey little fella"
"Hi" I said, in a squeky voce.
"wat do you want to day."
"Something" I replide
My mom said, "he want's some thing that walks and can fit in his tank." We walk down a huge iall. I look up and see cage's, fish, dog's. And thier it was. A little ity, bity, Iguana. The way he moved his head made me laugh. The guy say:
"Is that wat you want"
"Yes: I said, my mom said well take it. I starte Jumping wit joy. He brang it down. I started to pick it up. we went home and put it in the tank.

When looking at student work, it is helpful to recognize students' strengths in addition to looking for where they may be struggling. In seeing what they can do, we can also see what they are ready to learn. The following are some of the strengths we noticed and the implications for teaching that stemmed from these observations:

Student Strengths	Implications for Teaching
Dialogue included	Encourage consistent use in writer's notebooks during drafting phase
Dialogue tags	Share examples as a model for other students

Student Strengths	Implications for Teaching
Dialogue punctuated: new speaker, new line; spoken words inside quotation marks; commas	Conference with student in order to support conscious decision making during the writing process
Suspense built using a short sentence ("*I look up and see cage's, fish, dog's. And thier it was.*")	Include on rubric
Apostrophe use; sometimes connected to the letter *s*	Apostrophe instruction
Verbs have different and sometimes irregular forms in the past tense	Instruction around verb tense and subject–verb agreement

In order to further break down the grammatical errors, it can be helpful to create a chart like this (more assessment charts are included in Appendix A):

Errors in Written Academic Language	Implications for Teaching
"He say" (instead of "He says")	Subject–verb agreement
Apostrophe misuse (*mom's eye's; he want's; cage's; thats old enough*)	Apostrophe use: possession, contractions—no apostrophes for plurals
Verb tense ("*We walk . . . their it was*")	Past, present, and future verb forms
Verb form (*brang*)	Verb forms and conjugations
Ending punctuation ("*So I walk in. this huge guy . . .* "; missing periods)	Sentence structure
Fragments ("*A little, itty, bitty, Iguana.*")	Sentence structure
Paragraph (no indentations)	Paragraphing
Homophones ("*their it was*")	Homophone spelling
Other spelling errors (*wit* for *with*; *wat* for *what*; *voce* for *voice*; *replide* for *replied*; *iall* for *aisle*)	Other spelling rules

From these lists, we saw that there were many lessons that we needed to teach directly. We have designed these lessons for instruction outside of writing workshop because they are lessons aimed at teaching accurate conventions rather than lessons of craft. Though the lists can seem overwhelming, we saw that the lessons could fall into units of study: apostrophe use, homophones, and plural spelling rules. The order of the units seemed to matter; each unit supports the unit that follows. We also saw that errors like double negatives, verb forms, and conjugations needed to be addressed differently because those errors come directly from linguistic patterns. A unit on what we call everyday and academic language would then come next.

You can do this same work: Working with a colleague if you can, on your own if that is not possible, take a look at some samples of your students' writing. There are different ways and purposes for choosing which students' work to look at. Trying to look at every student's writing would take too much time, so you will want to gather a sample. One option is to choose "high," "medium," and "low" samples: a couple of students who you consider to write very well, a couple who are not yet as skilled, and a couple who you think really struggle. Another option is to choose several pieces written by students who you think fall pretty much in the middle—not the most or least adept, but ones you think match the way a lot of your students write. Read through the pieces and jot down the errors you notice. This will help you to decide which lessons you need to teach. We've included a form for taking these notes that may help in looking at student work in Appendix A. If your students' errors are similar to our students, you may be able to just follow our lesson sequence as presented in Chapters 4 and 5.

Looking at student work will give you an idea of what to include in whole-class and/or small-group lessons. When looking at student work, you get a good sense of how many students need particular instruction. Some errors in academic language seem to be ones that most of your students make; apostrophe misuse was one of those errors for our students. If most or all of your students are making particular errors in Standard English, it makes sense to make those whole-class lessons. If the majority of students seem to have mastery of a particular skill, but a select few do not, then it makes sense to teach just those select students in a small group. The "i before e" spelling rule was one of those for our students. There was a handful of students in our classes who routinely misspelled words like *piece*, but the majority of them followed the rule correctly. So, during sustained writing time during writing workshop, we gathered those students to a table set aside for just that purpose and taught that rule, while the others wrote independently. If only one student needs support with something a one-on-one conference with that student is probably the best approach. By getting to know your students as writers, your teaching becomes differentiated, truly addressing the needs of the individual students.

Deciding When and How to Do This Work

Reviewing student work with a colleague or colleagues is extraordinarily helpful. Depending on the structure of your school, you can work with a colleague who teaches the same grade and subject or one who teaches the same subject but in a different grade. In addition, having a literacy coach or administrator there as well can further everyone's perspectives. Working collaboratively allows for multiple sets of eyes to see with different perspectives. We would often notice different things, increasing the validity of the work.

Making time to look at student work and discuss students' oral language together is crucial. There are so many things as teachers that we want to do, but unless there is consistent time carved out of our schedules to do them, they would rarely get done. We'd like to offer some suggestions for when time can be made for this work. Twice a week for ninety minutes we met to plan our curriculum. We committed to looking at student work before and after the beginning of each writing unit. We allowed thirty minutes to do this work. At East Side, at the end of each teaching unit, our administration allows us to work a full day in the school reflecting on the last unit and planning the upcoming one. As the literacy coach, Elisa met with teachers on their planning days and encouraged them to bring in samples of student work so that each planning day began with looking at student work. If your school has vertical or department meetings, create time for reviewing student work. Looking at student work at the beginning of a unit helps to inform what lessons should be taught, and looking at the end helps to assess what the students learned and what they can do either habitually or during editing. It is also a critical time when we are honest about whether our students' work shows evidence of growth as a result of our teaching. This time allows us to recognize which areas of instruction need more support through reteaching or exploring areas of weakness in a different way. Don't be shy about being vocal about the importance of this work: It's an authentic and crucial form of data collection; it allows for looking at work in formative ways as opposed to only summative ways when it's time to grade; and, most important, it increases the potential for student achievement.

3

Planning Curricula and Creating Time to Include the Teaching of Grammar

Listening to our students and studying their writing unveiled two major ideas about our students' knowledge of written language. First, oral language heavily influenced our students' choices when they wrote. Our students' speech patterns—influenced by families, neighborhoods, the media, and even Spanish—affected how our students wrote. So, when we heard our students say, "I don't got no homework," we could anticipate and indeed saw a similar pattern in their writing. Learning this fact was critical as it taught us that our students did not always make haphazard guesses to grammar when writing. Rather, their writing organically came from patterns they already practiced when they spoke.

Following this trend, our second realization was that some factors in written language, like spelling rules and apostrophe use, held no significance in oral language. Truly, one simply does not need to differentiate between the spelling and apostrophe use in words like *your* and *you're* when speaking. In fact, apostrophe use and misuse, as well as homophone spelling errors, were some of the most glaring and distracting errors in our students' writing. It was clear that our students had learned that writers use apostrophes. Many students used them, but would throw them in any time they wrote the letter *s*. Thus, every plural was plagued with an apostrophe, while many contractions and words showing possession were left wanting. This is what we figured out: Many of their homophone misspellings were connected to misunderstandings about apostrophe use. Take *there*, *their*, and *they're*, or *its* and *it's*. Students did not consistently use the correct rules here. For example, they would write, "There dogs were barking" or "Its not my fault." We realized that if they understood the rules for apostrophe use, it would be easier to teach homophone spelling.

This process of looking together at our students' writing to understand why they were making the errors they were was invaluable to us because it helped us frame our grammar instruction. It wasn't just about helping students gain a rule that would replace what they already knew. From studying our students' writing and understanding what our students already knew about written language, our premise behind teaching academic language would include helping students gain an understanding of the language that grants access to the culture of power, one that may have different codes than their own. Bourdieu (1986) defines *cultural capital* as forms of knowledge, skill, and education that give a person higher status in society. The addition of these codes and the knowledge of when and how to use them (code-switching) is the kind of capital that would enable students to be successful in school, in college, and in mainstream society. The process also helped us envision a sequence for instruction. While gathering data about our students' written abilities, we identified some general areas where the majority of our students struggled, including homophones, apostrophes, plural spelling, subject–verb agreement (and verb forms in general), and double negatives. As described earlier, the first three areas are completely intertwined. To address these issues without context and connection, our students would continue to be confused by the mysteries of academic language. In our minds, we segmented what we learned into two areas: errors specific to writing and code-switching in speaking and writing.

In this curriculum, our students not only learned the rules of conventional grammar but also the language to use when talking about the writing decisions they were making. They no longer called the apostrophe "the comma up there," and they could name how and when to use one. We followed this with plural spelling rules since it connected directly to our students' misuse of the apostrophe and would reinforce their practice of using them correctly, and not using them whenever they wrote a plural. All of our units were designed like this. Teaching indefinite pronouns had to be taught with double negatives and code-switching; some verb conjugations had to accompany subject–verb agreement. Thus, we designed a cumulative approach so that an understanding of one area would help students understand the next.

Planning Backward

Developing a cumulative approach to teaching grammar was also rooted in our approach to curriculum design at East Side. For *all* of our units of study, we ask ourselves, what do we want our students to get out of doing this? Grant Wiggins' and Jay McTighe's (2005) work on helping teachers develop curriculum that ensures understanding—and not merely knowing—has helped us get to the heart of what we want our students to learn and be able to do as a result of each unit that we teach. Their approach to curriculum design, Understanding by Design (UbD), emphasizes backward planning, which suggests that teachers constantly keep in mind the ultimate goals of content, strategies, and ideas as they plan each individual lesson. By considering the destination, teachers can see clearly their teaching path along with the rationale for each lesson they choose to instruct. Instead of going with what we know best, Wiggins' and McTighe's work has helped us consider what we want our students to know in order to fulfill a unit's or lesson's objective. Backward planning has helped us keep a steady balance between where our students are and where we would like them ultimately to go.

The Understanding by Design (UbD) framework pushed us to think carefully about what we wanted students to get out of each unit, lesson, and assessment we introduced to our class. To make backward planning a mainstay in our curriculum design, we use planning sheets that feature overall course and unit goals, essential questions, and specific skills, strategies, or aspects of content we expect our students to learn for every aspect of Humanities. Thinking first about big ideas and understandings, as well as essential content and questions, allowed us to stay on the path of providing rigorous, thoughtful instruction to our students every day. Instead of keeping a narrow focus on what to prepare for individual, disconnected lessons, planning units under the UbD framework pushed us to keep the end in sight and help us consider how each student and teaching task was related to the overall goal of the unit. We came to understand that if a lesson did not help students better connect to the essential questions and ideas, then most likely it was not worth introducing to our class. Eventually, we added a "grammar" box to each planning sheet that reminded us to devise ways for constant transfer and application from the short grammar lessons to longer parts of class, like reading and writing. See the Appendix B for a blank UbD planning sheet and one that we completed for our Essay unit.

The UbD planning sheets also encapsulate the way we approach instruction and learning. When we plan an assignment or a lesson, we generally think first about what we want our students to get out of it, and we actually try to say that in one or two sentences in order to stay focused on only one objective. Thinking of a grammar lesson might lead us to say, "We want our students to know that there are many purposes of apostrophes. One of these is that they are used for contractions by taking the place of dropped letters when combining two words." Once we can articulate our goal, we now know our task is to develop lessons that will enable students to arrive at the original objective. It keeps the work of developing such lessons simple, focused, and purposeful.

Scheduling Time for the Grammar Curriculum

Even though the decision to develop simple and direct lessons was well informed, we immediately wondered how we would have the time to include it in an already full curriculum that we did not want to entirely overhaul. Indeed, we understood our limited amount of time, just two short hours a day in our Humanities classes, to be the very reason why we steered away from teaching grammar in the first place. Our past experiences taught us that allowing grammar instruction to dominate the curriculum would only waste time because a skills-based, isolated approach would be minimally effective in transferring necessary skills and strategies to authentic writing experiences. We understand that in an absence of a meaningful context, grammar holds no power for students. In fact, it could only become powerful when students had a real place to apply what they knew to what they were writing. Thus, students could still continue to construct their understanding about the power of writing even if our lessons were short and small. However we planned to teach grammar would have to find a real place in connection to writing workshop.

This time around, we would have to reconsider how we used time in our classrooms. It wasn't that we needed more time to teach grammar, but that we needed to use the time better. While holding sacred the major routines and rituals of our class time—independent reading and reading workshop minilessons, writing workshop, and social studies—we agreed that a fifteen-minute block dedicated to grammar three times a week could be effective so long as we planned that time well. We would have a total of forty-five minutes a week to introduce new concepts in grammar, model them, and leave some time for independent mastery. This short span of time, therefore, could not be a time for discovery, turning and talking, or elaborated reflection. This time would be devoted solely to giving students the tools they needed to improve their writing in Standard Written English. We liked the idea of shorter lessons, three times a week, instead of a one-shot weekly experience so that the students could appreciate the notion that mastering grammar would come with frequent and cumulative practice. Figure 3–1 shows a sample schedule in Humanities that includes three grammar lessons.

The flow of our class time relies heavily on structure, routines, and rituals. For example, the students understand that every day, when they enter the room, they will record on their reading logs the number of pages in their independent reading books that they read the night before, take out their book from their bookbags, and read silently for the next thirty minutes. We believe that this structure is helpful for students to learn the importance of routines and practice, and we also believe that it helps students get prepared for class. Following this approach, our grammar lessons would have to become an expected ritual in class as well, so we inserted the fifteen minutes right before writing workshop every Tuesday, Wednesday, and Thursday. Ostensibly, knowing when and for how long each grammar lesson would occur was extremely useful for planning the lessons.

Monday	Tuesday	Wednesday	Thursday	Friday
Reading Workshop: Minilesson (10–15 minutes) Independent Reading (30 minutes) Writing Workshop: Minilesson (10–15 minutes) Independent Writing (30 minutes)	Reading Workshop Grammar Lesson Writing Workshop	Independent Reading Read-Aloud Grammar Lesson Writing Workshop	Independent Reading Read-Aloud Grammar Lesson Writing Workshop	Reading Workshop Writing Workshop

figure 3–1 Sample Humanities Schedule of Grammar Instruction

PART

The Grammar Curriculum

4

Designing the Grammar Lessons and Developing Lessons on Inaudible Errors

Apostrophes, Homophones, and Plural Nouns

Our existing instructional and planning features laid a strong foundation for designing a grammar curriculum. In this chapter, we explain the components of a typical grammar lesson. You can reproduce the lesson and state the rule exactly as we have it here, although we think it is more powerful for teachers to make slight changes in the examples and sentences for practice. When you personalize the examples and sentences for practice, you can use words that support the vocabulary or content connected to your own curriculum, and you can include little interesting facts about yourself and your students that will make the examples and sentences intriguing to your particular students. (It's amazing how tucking in tidbits about your life or an event at school holds the students' attention and provides motivation and enjoyment.)

You'll see that the grammar lesson follows the typical minilesson structure developed by Lucy Calkins, which includes a connection, a teaching demonstration, an opportunity for active engagement or practice, and a link to students' ongoing work. The following is a brief explanation of how the grammar lessons tend to go:

1. The grammar rule is named, defined in one sentence, and is numbered. (We call it a *rule* because the grammar points we're teaching tend to be aspects of academic language that can either be correct or incorrect, depending on

usage.) This sentence may define a skill or convention, explain one of its purposes, or describe what it will look like when used appropriately. The sentence also uses the most relevant, accessible language to define and explain the skill or convention. We give students just enough academic language to use it in their writing, but we are cautious not to overload them with irrelevant definitions. For example, instead of *transitive* or *linking verb*, we'll just say *verb*. The immediate goal is not for a student to know the difference between a transitive or linking verb. In the short term, that may detract from the ultimate goal, which is to be able to use verbs correctly in an academic context.

2. Three model sentences are presented, each showing the correct usage of the rule. These sentences may also include correct usage of any previous rules they've learned, which enables us to constantly reinforce the lessons.

3. Next, we provide three sentences for practice. These sentences have errors or opportunities for the students to apply the new rule. In order to fix the sentences, they also must apply previous rules they have learned. We are careful to make sure that the errors in these practice sentences reflect the kinds of patterns we see in our students' writing.

4. We also add a few additional features to the model sentences and sentences for practice. We use these sentences to support our students' acquisition of sophisticated vocabulary by including new words they are learning. We incorporate bits of information about the teachers and the staff in order to make personal connections. Our students prefer these personalized sentences rather than those from a generic, traditional workbook because they appeal directly to their needs and interests.

5. In reviewing the corrections with the students, we ask them to name and explain each correction so that they would own the rules and the accompanying language.

These grammar lessons are designed so that they can be used for whole-class instruction, small-group work, or individual instruction. Each lesson is designed to be ten to fifteen minutes long, and teachers can choose to teach one to three rules per week. We aim for consistency across the grammar lessons by adhering to these characteristics (a reproducible version is located in Appendix C):

- Write the grammar or spelling rule in one sentence.

- Include examples of rules taught previously in model sentences and sentences for practice to strive for cumulative accountability.

- Use practice sentences that mirror patterns in student writing.

- Write the model sentences and sentences for practice in an order of increasing complexity. The more rules the students learn, the more cumulative and complex the sentences get.

- Include vocabulary or content information connected to the curriculum or fun facts about ourselves or the school in the sentences.

Here is a sample of how a grammar lesson on apostrophes went in our classes:

GETTING READY

Distribute (about 1–2 minutes)

Give each student a copy of the handout (this includes the grammar rule, examples of the rule used correctly, and sentences for practice). Students may either copy them into the conventions section of their writer's notebooks, a conventions notebook (a separate notebook kept for the grammar lessons), or keep it in a writing folder. We also put a copy of the handout on an overhead transparency, or have the rule, examples, and sentences for practice visible on the board. (Examples of handouts appear at the end of this section.)

GRAMMAR RULE MINILESSON

Connection (about 1 minute)

"So, you've learned two rules for using apostrophes already, and both are to show possession [*point to the* Grammar Rules You've Learned *poster* (see Figure 6–1)]. There is another rule for using apostrophes that I'm going to teach you today. That rule is for contractions. Sometimes when we speak and write, we combine two words to make our speech or writing sound smoother, faster, or more realistic. When we say 'Don't forget,' we're combining *do* and *not* into one word, *don't*. There is a specific rule for how to do this in writing. Let's see what it looks like."

Teaching and Demonstration (about 3–4 minutes)

"Everyone follow along as I read the rule aloud. Apostrophes are used for contractions—they take the place of dropped letters when combining two words. Take a look at the examples so you see what I mean here. [*Reading aloud.*] *It's raining outside so they're staying inside. It's* is short for *it is* [*circle or underline* It's *and write* it is *above it, so you are annotating as you explain*]. You are dropping the letter *i*, so that is where you place the apostrophe. The apostrophe takes the place of the dropped letter. Let's keep going. [*Reading aloud.*] *It's raining outside so they're staying inside.* [*Underline* they're.] If you slow that down when you say it, you see that you are saying *they are* [*go ahead and annotate that part*]. The apostrophe goes between the *y* and the *r* because it is taking the place of the dropped letter *a*." [*Continue and follow the same format for the next two examples. Make sure to point out that in the third example, the apostrophe takes the place of two dropped letters—both the* w *and the* i *for* he'll.]

Active Engagement/Practice (about 5–8 minutes)

"Now I want you to practice. Go ahead and make the necessary corrections on the practice sentences. Remember: You are looking for words that need apostrophes for contractions and for possession as well. You are practicing using all the rules you've learned so far." [*Possible modifications: You can write the number of errors that appear in each sentence on the lefthand side of each sentence: 1 next to #1, 3 next to #2, and 2 next to #3. That way, the students know how many errors they are looking for. We sometimes gave the number of errors for the first one or two and left sentence 3 unmarked. For specific students, often those with IEPs, we wrote the numbers on their papers. You can circulate here, assisting those who need it.*]

After a bit of time, you may want to have your students share some of the work they did on the sentences with each other. We often travel around the classroom and listen in as students are talking to each other to see how the work has gone. Once they've shared with each other for a few minutes, we bring everyone back together and go over each of the practice sentences, inviting participation and using the terminology of the lessons.

Link to Ongoing Work (about 1 minute)

"So now you know two instances when you can use apostrophes—to show possession and for contractions. I'm going to teach you the third and last rule for using apostrophes next lesson. I'm expecting to see you using apostrophes for possession and contractions in all the writing that you do from now on. Everyone will be able to edit for apostrophes, and some of you will be able to start using them when you are working in your notebooks or on your drafts during writing workshop. Each one of you showed today that you understood this rule. So now that you know the rule, it's up to you to actively use it in your writing. You can always look at the Grammar Rules You've Learned poster or in your notebook to remind yourself what the rule is and to see an example of it. I'll be looking today and every day as we write to see how you are doing with this work."

Because the lessons are short, you may be able to photocopy three different lessons per page, making your photocopying load lighter and saving paper in the process. We suggest that students have a place, either a conventions notebook or a writing folder, where they can accumulate the grammar lessons. During writing workshop, we urge them to keep their convention notebook or writing folder handy and to use it as a resource as they write.

All the lessons follow this same format. They all last fifteen minutes or less. The more rules students learn, the more cumulative and complex the sentences get. For the minilesson, we strongly recommend that you have an enlarged copy of the lesson, either showing on an overhead projector, a document camera, or written on the board because it's important that all eyes are on the same text.

Depending on how often you want to fold this grammar work into your teaching schedule—one, two, or three times each week—you might decide to have a quick review day as well. If you want to teach one rule a week, say on Mondays, you could have a quick review on Thursdays or Fridays. Just write up one to three sentences for practice, and have that be the only part of the lesson, taking about five to seven minutes. You could also have students write sentences for practice and swap with a partner.

A Plan for Instruction on Apostrophes, Homophones, and Plural Spellings

The following is the sequence for our grammar lessons. While these lessons share a similar format, we approach instruction about apostrophes, homophones, and plural spellings differently than the way we approach lessons on code-switching (which will be covered in the Chapter 5). The first group—apostrophes, homophones, and plural spelling—relates more to tangible errors of academic language that we notice in our students' writing. It also involves naming features of the language, explaining their function, and teaching students how to use them in their writing. When we introduce our lessons that are connected to code-switching in the next chapter, we acknowledge that some of these writing issues relate to our students' understanding of who they are, how they speak, and the way they write and the lessons may be different for those reasons.

Our suggested sequence for teaching apostrophes, homophones, and plural spellings was developed by noticing and naming some of the most urgent and common needs we observed in our students' raw and formal writing. We have included ideas for student investigation and quizzes in this section as well, and, in Chapter 6, we will elaborate on these and other forms of assessment. By looking at your own students' work, you may identify some other areas that you think are worth addressing.

Teaching About Inaudible Errors: Apostrophes, Homophones, and Plural Spelling

We originally wanted to begin the grammar instruction with lessons on homophones. The confusion of homophones was particularly rampant in our students' writing and it caused some of the most distracting errors. We wanted to begin with what was most distracting to the reader and work from there. When studying our students' writing, however, we saw that homophone errors were directly linked to errors in apostrophe use. Many students clearly knew that writers use apostrophes, but they tended to add them whenever they used the letter *s*, plaguing plural nouns with them. We realized that in order to understand the spelling of homophones like *there, their,* and *they're,* or to know not to add an apostrophe to a plural, it was essential to understand apostrophe use for possession, contractions, and other dropped letters. So that is where we started.

These lessons, along with the lessons on plural spelling rules, are all inaudible errors; they have no connection to oral language whatsoever. Some factors in written language, like spelling rules and apostrophe use, hold no significance in oral language. It is impossible to differentiate between the spelling and apostrophe use in words like *its* and *it's* when speaking. Mistakes in apostrophe use, and homophone and plural spelling are all truly errors in academic language. Unlike in code-switching rules, there is never a context in which different usage is acceptable. Thus, these lessons are not about choice, but about understanding and learning specific rules.

Evidence of Student Progress

Before going any further, we wanted to share some examples of our students' growth because of this curriculum. It's important to remember that these changes took place not over the course of a week or two, but across several months. Because the sentences for practice are cumulative and there are connections made in reading and writing workshop and beyond, students are revisiting areas of struggle again and again, helping their new learning to become habitual. As we all know, new habits are not formed quickly, but need consistent practice and multiple contexts in which to practice them.

Read the following student excerpts written before and after grammar instruction:

Before Grammar Instruction (bold italics show errors in apostrophe use, homophones, and plural spelling)	After Grammar Instruction (bold italics show growth in areas in which students previously struggled)
We learned to be powerful *reader's* . . . You have to keep a reading record of the *book's* that you read throughout the year. Also you have to keep another record *wich* is a list of *book's* that you have completed because that *keep's* you organized. (Rynetta)	The thing I learned about grammar is that the *apostrophes* in the *words* are used for *contractions*. Also they take *places* of *dropped letters* when you combine two words. Example: *It's* raining today so *they're* staying outside. That is the correct way of doing it but we had to correct *sentences* that *don't* have *apostrophes*. (Rynetta)
If two people are in love why can't they honor *there* love and get married. I don't understand this world. I really don't. Long ago *black* were *slave* even though *there* are not *their* still racism against them and now gay people can't get married. Blacks were treated badly because of the their color and *gay's* are treated different because of the way they are. Are we expected to be the same? (Esther)	Then *there's* Mr. Powell who also wants Beth . . . but once they get started with *their* study *sessions* she *starts* to see what a "great" person he is. . . . (Esther)
He *didnt* even give peace a chance. He got us into a war. He got *thousand's* of people killed. . . . He *cant* find Osama Bin Laden either. This *show's* how. . . . (Christopher)	Most of my *poems* are *connections* to the world, and *others* are connections to the way I see *things* and what *I've* been through in the past, like Tupac Shakur*'s* Untitled poem. (Christopher)

Before Grammar Instruction (bold italics show errors in apostrophe use, homophones, and plural spelling)	After Grammar Instruction (bold italics show growth in areas in which students previously struggled)
I hated feeling like a criminal in my home and *friends* house. One night I came home after school. I walked across East Houston Street and thought *whats* gonna happen to me. Oohh I knew I should have left earlier, but I was having fun. Okay Okay I'll just speed walk so I *wont* be extremely late but I know it *wont* make a difference. (Kenya)	I used the stanza strategy so my poem *wouldn't* look like a huge paragraph. You *don't* treat me with respect You always question who *I'm* on the phone with You make me think you *don't* want to be with me (Kenya)

As you can see from the excerpts on the left, the students' use of apostrophes, homophones, and plural spelling rules is inconsistent. They all know that writers use apostrophes, and that they sometimes are connected to the letter *s*. They also have a sense that words like *there* have different spellings. Without an understanding of when and how to use these differences, they become a real distraction for the reader.

Lessons on Apostrophes, Homophones, and Plural Noun Spelling

Following is the sequence of lessons for inaudible errors. The lessons are presented in a particular order, described earlier in this chapter, which allows each lesson to build on the ones that came before. Notice how each lesson follows the same format, how the errors in the sentences for practice mirror the errors students make in their own writing, and how the sentences are cumulative, building in continued and consistent practice of rules learned.

Apostrophes

GRAMMAR RULE #1: Apostrophes are used to show possession. If the noun is singular, add **'s** to the noun.

Examples:

- Chantal's water bottle. (*Chantal is the owner, or possesses the water bottle. It belongs to her.*)
- The student's desk is clean.
- The dog's tail wagged when Kathleen returned home.

Sentences for Practice:

1. She accidentally stepped on Chantals glasses.
2. Andres teacher was impressed with his compelling essay.
3. Kathleen pencil broke.

GRAMMAR RULE #2: For plural nouns or any noun ending in **s**, add an apostrophe after the **s**.

Examples:

- The students' grades improved in the second semester.
- Elisa got the class' attention.
- The butterflies' wings were flapping all around us at the museum.

Sentences for Practice:

1. The eighth graders bake sale raised $100.
2. What is Chris phone number?
3. East Sides reputation is growing because of all of our visitors feedback.

GRAMMAR RULE #3: Apostrophes are used for *contractions*—they take the place of dropped letters when combining two words.

Examples:

- It's raining today so they're staying inside.
- He didn't bring Kathleen's umbrella.
- He'll apologize tomorrow.

Sentences for Practice:

1. She cant go to the dance on Friday.
2. Chantals camera wasnt working because its broken.
3. The students voices are loud because there excited.

GRAMMAR RULE #4: Apostrophes are used in place of dropped letters at the beginnings and ends of words.

Examples:

- Some students prefer chillin' after school to doing homework.
- Chantal's nephew was sittin' under the tree.
- "Let's get goin'!"

Sentences for Practice:

1. The naughty boy averted his eyes and said, "Im not doin anything."
2. Elisas head ached cause she was tired.
3. In order to expedite the process, Kathleen quit relaxin on her friends couch.

Opportunity for Student Investigations • We think it's vital for students to also notice and investigate the use of the grammar rules themselves, finding places in texts where authors have used the rules they are learning. Once students are familiar with a few grammar rules, we show them how to investigate the usage of the rule in published texts. Students might create a chart like the one that follows in their conventions notebook or keep it in their writing folder to hold the work of their investigations. (Chapter 6 details the investigation process, as well as other extensions that will make what students learn in these lessons last well beyond the moment of the lesson.)

Student Investigation Chart

Examples of Grammar Rule	Symbol/Name/ Purpose	What It Means	My Turn to Try It!
It's time to go.	'/apostrophe (for contraction)	It is	Don't forget me.

It isn't our intention to interfere with our students' reading work by having them fill in this chart as they read. Instead, we might provide time, five minutes or so, at the end of reading workshop a couple of times a week for students to go back into their independent reading texts to find places where authors applied the grammar rules we are learning. Alternatively, we could ask students to do some of this investigation work for homework a couple of times a week.

GRAMMAR RULE #5: Exceptions: Apostrophes are *not* used to show possession with pronouns (*my, his, her, our, their, its*).

Examples:

- The dog got its tail stuck in the door.
- They averted their eyes from the bright sun.
- My friend's mother gave us our afternoon snack.

Sentences for Practice:

1. What were the boys thinking when they forgot there lunches?
2. The class had it's picture taken quickly to expedite the process.
3. That was hour soda but there going to say its theres.

Grammar Rules Quiz: Apostrophes*

PART ONE

Correct the following sentences.

1. Her friends brother asked, "Where are you goin after school?"

2. The students know its the 15th of February and there prone to counting the days until vacation.

3. The students teachers reminded them to avert they're eyes during the quiz.

4. There kitten was adorable when it put its paw in Chantals cup of milk.

5. Kathleen followed her intuition when she decided she didnt want to go to her friends birthday party.

CHALLENGE SENTENCE—EXTRA CREDIT:

My friends mothers baby cries when its noisy, when it's bottle is empty, and when their eating there dinner.

PART TWO

Write a paragraph that includes at least one example of each of the following five grammar rules you've learned:

1. Singular possessive

2. Plural possessive

3. Contractions

4. Dropped letters

5. Possessive pronouns

Possible topics for your paragraph:

- Your favorite movie/book/video game

- What you plan to do over break next week

- The new school start time

- Other persuasive topic

* See Appendix E for a modified version of this quiz.

Homophones

First you'll want to define the word *homophone*. We always pointed to the two parts of the word to explain that *homo* means same, and *phone* means sound. Also, you can start the investigation work right away here, and as you teach more, they'll investigate more homophones.

> *Homophones:* Words that sound the same but have different spellings and meanings (e.g, *two/too/to* and *your/you're*).

GRAMMAR RULE #6: Homophones: *two* (the number 2), *too* (also or very), *to* (if it's not either of the others, then use *to*).

Examples:

- There are two cupcakes on Elisa's desk.
- Kathleen wanted a cupcake too.
- Chantal ate too much pizza so her stomach ached.
- Mark went to their classrooms to see what the students were up to.

Sentences for Practice:

1. They ordered to pizzas to go on their way home.
2. There are to many kids outside who need too be home.
3. When they got too there apartment, they said, "Were coming to!"

Student Investigation Work ● We used a chart that looked like this:

Example from Text	Homophone	What the Homophone Means
I've got some stuff to do, too.	too	also

GRAMMAR RULE #7: Homophones: *their* (shows possession), *they're* (contraction: they are), *there* (location/place or if it's *not* either of the others).

Examples:

- Kathleen and Elisa wanted their students to do their homework.

- They're prone to following their intuition.

- Chantal's brother went there yesterday.

Sentences for Practice:

1. The students felt timid when they saw they're new teacher.

2. There is no need to belittle people when their different than you.

3. Elisas class believed their were good reason's to start completing all there homework.

GRAMMAR RULE #8: Homophones: *it's* (contraction: it is) and *its* (possessive pronoun).

Examples:

- It's almost the end of the semester.

- The dog chased its tail.

Sentences for Practice:

1. I heard Jose say, "Lets stay after school to finish our project before its too late."

2. Kathleens baby was compelled by it's reflection in the mirror's around the house.

3. It's up to Ileana to decide if you can hand in you're science report's tomorrow. Either way, its time to finish em up.

GRAMMAR RULE #9: Homophones: *you're* (contraction: you are) and *your* (possessive pronoun).

Examples:

- You're the student of the month.

- It's your responsibility to walk your dog.

Sentences for Practice:

1. You're going to think it's not you're problem.

2. Your feeling anxious today because of your math test.

3. Your the student who like's to take all the teachers attendance folder's down to the main office, so you consider it you're job.

Since students were not learning a new rule, but needed continued practice with homophones, they created their own definitions or examples in the next lesson. We followed this with adding Sentences for Practice, which allowed the lessons and cumulative practice to remain consistent.

Other Common Homophones	
Directions: Write the definition or an example of the following homophones.	

Homophone	Definition/Example
peace	
piece	
knew	
new	
by	
buy	
bye	
mail	
male	
know	
no	
scent	
sent	
cent	
whole	
hole	
would	
wood	
write	
right	
through	
threw	
wait	
weight	
where	
wear	
not	
knot	
steel	
steal	

The first set of Sentences for Practice could be used in class, and the second set as homework.

Sentences for Practice:

1. Elisa new she had to bye flower before she made her delectable cookie's. After they were done, she exclaimed, "There ready!"

2. Even the timid student's edited there political letters with fervor because they new the letter's were being maled soon.

Sentences for Practice:

1. Write before the last out, you threw the ball with fervor to home plate, but, cause your prone to overdoing it, the ball went saling threw there window.

2. The federal judge read the students letter suggesting that the Supreme Court consider making same-sex marriage legal for the hole country, and not to weight for state court's to agree on the issue, because, the student argued, its the write thing to do.

Homophones Quiz Practice

When I grow up I am going to bee a superstar! My plan is two study four for years at the Performing Arts High School in Manhattan. During the first too years I will study as a dancer. I herd the program at they're school is wonderful for dancing, but their real tough on you. For example they don't let you eat any meet during the weak, only on the weekends! They say that so I won't gain any more wait. But once you go threw the program, your given the opportunity to perform in a video that will bee on MTV. How Exciting! I'm going to ask all my friends to by the video on DVD. After the first couple of years, I'll participate in the acting pro-gram. The toughest part of this program is that I'll have to right and perform in my own play. And I'll have to attend schools for nine ours a day! The principle told me that I Have a good change of getting a part in a soap opera if I do well at this school. Wow! You know what they say about New York—if I can make it their, I can make it anywear!

Homophones Quiz*

PART ONE

Directions: Edit the following paragraphs by circling the incorrect words and writing the correct spelling above the word. The first one has been underlined and corrected as an example. There are ten errors in each paragraph (twenty total).

                         Women's
March is <u>Womens</u> History Month. We would like you all to try and read one or two books about girl's who have made a difference or books by women author's as a way to celebrate and learn something knew. As you know, women didnt get the right to vote until the nineteenth amendment was added to the Constitution in 1920. Before 1920, there were to women who didn't avert there eye's from that prejudice: Elizabeth Cady Stanton and Susan B. Anthony. They fought hard to allow women they're right to vote. Although women have made a lot of progress, our country is not doing it's best. We have never had a female president, but womens intuition tells us that will change soon.

On another note, all of your teacher's are hoping that you'll think about homophones every time you put your pen to paper. We no teenager's are prone to writing to quickly, so we want you to always reread you're writing slowly to check for error's. Otherwise, all these rule's you've learned wont ever become habits. That would be ideal and we hope your ready for that. And don't forget: Use the words of the week in your sentence's in the next part and get extra credit!

PART TWO

Directions: Choose five word pairs and two write sentences that use the words correctly (ten sentences in total).

their, they're	it's, its	your, you're	through, threw	not, knot
steel, steal	knew, new	where, wear	right, write	scent, sent
wood, would	by, buy	no, know	mail, male	peace, piece

1a._____

1b._____

2a._____

2b._____

* See Appendix E for the modified paragraphs for Part 1 of the Homophones Quiz.

```
3a._____

3b._____

4a._____

4b._____

5a._____

5b._____
```

Plural Spelling Rules

In Appendix D, you will find a chart of the plural spelling rules. This is meant to be a resource for the teacher; you may want to review them or choose alternate rules to teach.

Note: A helpful tip to add when sharing this next rule came from a student: You know you have to add *–es* instead of just *–s* because you can't say the words out loud without adding the extra syllable when they are plural (e.g., box*es*).

GRAMMAR RULE #10: To make a singular (one) noun plural (more than one), add an *–s* at the end of the word. But for words that end in *sh, ch, x,* and *z*, add an *–es* to the end of the word. **Never add an apostrophe to make a plural noun!**

Examples:

* All studen**ts** are expected to straighten their des**ks** at the end of class.

* In order for my mentor to get to know me better, we have four delectable lun**ches** planned this month.

Sentences for Practice:

1. Witchs are prone to adding toxin's into they're soups.

2. Elisas least favorite chore is washing dishs at the end of the day.

3. When I go to the store, I must remember too by toothpickses, boxs, matchs, and two shirt's.

Note: For this unit, like for the homophones unit, it's helpful to start the investigations after introducing the first rule, and then have students build their charts from there. The investigations would be continuous throughout this study. A chart for this unit could look like this:

Example from Text	Singular Noun	Plural Noun
A few inches above the ground.	inch	inches

GRAMMAR RULE #11: When a singular noun ends in a consonant and then a *y*, change the *y* to an *i* and add *–es* to make it plural. When a singular noun ends in a vowel and then a *y*, just add an *–s* to make it plural. **Never add an apostrophe to make a plural noun!**

Examples:

- Both Carla and Erika have had ba**bies** in the past year.
- Pepe the custodian has k**eys** to open every door at East Side.

Sentences for Practice:

1. Gary is a wonderful mentor because he helps many student's with there studys.

2. Its unbelievable that student's have off two dayes next weak so that they're teacher's can expedite grading the math test!

3. When your in the tenth grade at East Side, you will probably right too short storys.

GRAMMAR RULE #12: When a singular noun ends in a vowel and then an *o* (*radio*), just add an *–s* to make it plural (*radios*). If it ends in a consonant and then an *o* (*tornado*), add *–es* (*tornadoes*) to make it plural.* **Never add an apostrophe to make a plural noun!**

Examples:

- Kangar**oos** are prone to hopping.

- He**roes** don't avert their eyes from trouble.

Sentences for Practice:

1. The yoga studioes were all pleasant, but one was ideal because of it's location.

2. Chantals' potatos were delectable because of there flavor.

3. The tornados location was broadcast over everyones radio's to expedite there evacuation.

*An exception to the rule is zero: one zero, two zeros.

GRAMMAR RULE #13: When the plural of a singular noun ending in *f*, *fe*, or *lf* (*chief*) has an *f* sound, just add *–s* to make it plural (*chiefs*). When the plural has a *v* sound, change the *f* to *v* and add *–es* (*wife* to *wives*). **Never add an apostrophe to make a plural noun!**

Examples:

- The *chefs* had a cooking contest.

- *Leaves* fall from trees in autumn.

Sentences for Practice:

1. Ideally, they're lifes will be happy and successful.

2. Kathleens delectable tomatos fell off of her kitchen shelfs.

3. The thiefs intuition told them not to rob the fresh berrys from there friends store and to put there knifes away for good.

GRAMMAR RULE #14: The plural form of some nouns are made in irregular ways:

foot/*feet*   man/*men*   woman/*women*   child/*children*   mouse/*mice*
tooth/*teeth*   crisis/*crises*   fish/*fish* or *fishes*

Never add an apostrophe to make a plural noun!

Examples:

- Chantal's nephew just lost his two front teeth.
- After the attic was doused with toxic chemicals, the mice scurried out of the window.

Sentences for Practice:

1. March was Womans History Month, but April is National Poetry Month.

2. Elisa had two crisises in March. First she couldnt find her grade book, and then she arrived late too her yoga class!

3. The bank robber yelled with fervor, "Its goin to be womans on this side, mens on the other!" and the victims ran too the sides of the room.

Grammar Quiz Practice

PART ONE

Directions: Edit the following paragraphs by circling the incorrect words and writing the correct spelling above the word. There are six to ten errors total.

Have You Read Any Storys About Animals?

Wolfs are found in many parts of the world and can live in many different habitats. They can live in prairies, forests, and mountains. A female wolf and her cubes may make a den (a home) in a cave, in a hole in the ground, or even in a hollow tree trunk. Wolves normally hunt small animals and birds and may also eat fruit such as berrys. However, wolves in a pack might even attack an animal as large as a reindeer or a sheep. People often fear wolves, but they shouldnt. Healthy wolves do not attack human's. Hunting and the clearing of forestes have driven wolves away from much of the western United States. People are now working to help bring wolves back into national parkes.

PART TWO

Directions: Write the plural form of the following words:

1. candy	7. woman
2. shirt	8. tooth
3. country	9. tornado
4. knife	10. library
5. glass	11. yourself
6. beach	12. box

Plural Spelling Quiz*

PART ONE (30 POINTS)

Directions: There are twenty errors that you need to fix. Circle each one. Note: There are ten errors in each paragraph.

In the middle of May, visitors from all around New York City will come to speak to East Side middle school students about they're careers. We teachers know that you may think that its too early for you too start thinking about what kind of job you will pursue in the future, but its a great idea for you to be exposed to the different opportunitys that you may have. We know that some of you want to have familys, right? Some girls may want to be wifes and have a few babys, and some boys want to grow up to be strong mans and lead powerful lifes, but you have to start thinking about what else is out there.

Some people simply choose a career based on how much money theyll make or how famous they will be. However, many people work in numerous fields doing fascinating activitys that youve never even heard of. People who love there jobs don't just do it for the money. Instead, they usually have a passion for their work and want to share that passion with other people. That passion may be about curing sick animal's, preparing delectable lunchs for the homeless, drawing and painting in art studioes, counseling people about their crisises, and, of course, even teaching childs. You don't need a cape or a flashy uniform to be great—as long as you care about your job, all of you could be heros!

PART TWO (20 POINTS)

Directions: On the lines provided, write ten sentences. In each sentence, you must use the plural form of one word in the word bank.

Word Bank							
woman	chief	key	mess	quiz	radio	potato	mouse
shoe	library	shelf	beach	watch	leaf	lady	child

1. _____

2. _____

* See Appendix E for the modified paragraphs for Part 1 of the Plural Spelling Quiz.

3. _____

4. _____

5. _____

6. _____

7. _____

8. _____

9. _____

10. _____

5

Developing Lessons on Code-Switching

Double Negatives, Subject–Verb Agreement,
and Additional Patterns Specific to Student Writing

For all of us, language is a window to our identity. We use it to articulate our experiences in the world (Gee 2001) and to communicate our hopes, desires, and angst to others. Because the way we speak reflects our identity, it is rare to find a person living in the United States who speaks a language that precisely mirrors all of the rules of Standard Written English.

As we write and talk in order to relate to others, our interactions with our friends and families, colleagues, and even the media influence how we communicate, and may ultimately influence how we communicate with a given audience. Because language represents power in our society, we need to be aware of and able to use a variety of discourse patterns, depending on our audience and context. After all, we know that the way we speak in some contexts differs from the way we write, as we have the agency to make informed choices so that we can communicate appropriately in academic settings. The choices we make around language use in a given setting grants us access and capital. Similarly, if we don't make choices around language use, or don't know what kinds of choices are appropriate for a given setting, we might be shut out of opportunities that we seek or ignored or undervalued.

We understood these ideas personally, and we saw these issues arise among our students. In order to prepare lessons for code-switching, we spent time reading our students' writing and identifying common areas where we saw reflections of oral language structures in their written pieces. We also continued to listen to our students—in class, in the cafeteria, at recess, and in the hallway—to hear the language structures that made up their everyday oral language patterns and features. Take a look at excerpts from some entries that Devonti composed in his writer's notebook. The parts in bold italics match his speech patterns.

> I teach other kids how to respect other people. I feel real good about my self and for that kid because *I'm pass on stuff my mom be teaching me. I some time be forgetting* I'm a kid myself the way I'm teaching these kids. *The teacher say* I'm a good kid. I'm am a good kid.

> *I seen* two kids named Herbie and Justice. it was a few years ago in 3rd grade. It was the first day of school. *I didn't know no one. We all was* little too. It was lunch time, We all go down stair to the lunch room. We all ate. I ate by myself because *I didn't know no one* at that time.

> I was walking with some of my friends and *we was joking.* Some of my friends saw a real black kid. So as we walk by every one was joking on him. *I did'nt say nothing* because my mom told me *not to make fun of no body for no reason.* I use to think that white *people was* scared of black because *I be whaching* movie when you see a black people all way making white people jump all the time.

In these excerpts, Devonti's writing accomplishes several things that good writers do all at once. He contemplates big issues, like loneliness, racism, and bullying, all through past experiences, and aims to express how those experiences impact who he is today. We read Devonti's writing like the way we hear him speak, and his strong sense of voice invites the reader into his world. In his writer's notebook, as a freewrite, this kind of writing works well as he practices the genre of narrative writing. Because this kind of writing is typical of what he produced in his writer's notebook, we wondered if he knew how to make the switch between everyday language and academic language. As teachers, we want Devonti to assert his voice, develop his narrative writing skills, and also learn how to communicate effectively with a wider audience. As Devonti continues to freewrite and starts drafting, we expect him to be aware not only of the choices that he can make in his writing but also to know what to do in his writing once he has made those choices. Writing this entire piece in academic language could very well be an appropriate step. But perhaps Devonti would become an even stronger writer if he considered which lines—those that show inner thinking? dialogue? certain details?—would demonstrate a strong sense of voice and still communicate effectively, even if he wrote them in everyday language.

In listening to our students and reading their writing, we realized that we might prevent our students from excelling academically if we did not encourage an awareness and practice of Standard English. At the same time, we respected our students' identities and wanted to build on to who they were instead of suggesting that the language that they brought to school was inadequate. To do this, Geneva Smitherman (1986) says that educators need to teach students "communicative competence" so that they make informed choices of language in academic and real-world contexts. This kind of competence includes skills that go beyond a knowledge of grammar and enables students to make choices of what language to use that is appropriate for the situation and the audience. Communicative competence also assumes a knowledge of who the audience is, what they want, and how they like to be addressed, as "these issues constitute language power" (Smitherman 1986, 229). This kind of knowledge will help students understand the norms of cultural identities that may be unlike their own and will give them an increased advantage to navigate among those identities. As students become better writers, they will begin to understand that not only is writing an act of communication but it is also an act of political and social power.

Given that schools may inadvertently perpetuate inequities instead of dismantle them, we believe that we have to do specific work with students so that they acquire the tools they need to navigate mainstream society successfully while simultaneously valuing their own identity and critically examining the structures in society that sustain inequality. Engaging in these three processes at the same time is tricky—how do you communicate with students the idea that even though it shouldn't be, one way of writing English has more power than others, and that we also want them to have the power to survive and question the way things are?

In thinking more about this question, we learned about Rebecca Wheeler and Rachel Swords' (2006) approach to teaching Standard English to students in urban schools. The two authors assert that the "errors" that teachers hear African American students make are actually speech patterns that reflect students' cultural identities. Thus, teachers can help their students build from what they already know to help them acquire the patterns of Standard English. The instructional method they use is *contrastive analysis*, a practice that allows students to compare and contrast the speech patterns in their home language to the speech patterns in Standard English. This instructional approach accomplishes two critical goals: encouraging teachers to appreciate the linguistic identity of their students, and allowing students to gain access to more standard forms of English strategically and metacognitively, without denigrating who they are. Much of our work in this section builds from Wheeler's and Swords' approach. In addition, we continue the pattern of grammar lessons established in Chapter 4 that frontloads students' learning with a rule, examples of the rule, and sentences for practice. We also offer possibilities to connect this instruction to students' writing workshop experiences.

Our writing workshop curriculum is designed to give students the tools and opportunities to critically examine daily and institutionalized forms of hurt, unfairness, and inequality. Writing workshop also provides them a forum to advocate for change, celebrate their own life experiences, and make their readers laugh. Our students have opportunities to write about personal experiences through their narratives about events with their families or the first time they encountered racism. Students additionally write editorials as well as business and political letters, on topics such as advocating for new laws on gay marriage to pressuring the governor to provide more funding to New York City schools. These genres provide students with opportunities to position themselves powerfully within and against the world; without these opportunities for critical examination in writing workshop, a curriculum that focuses on conventions would be meaningless. Teaching students about the differences between academic language and everyday language is larger than providing them with a one-sentence rule supported by examples. What precedes it must be a discussion about the norms of mainstream society. Specifically, we talk about the norms that often perpetuate inequalities that make it more difficult for urban, poor students of color to be successful in school. Here is what that kind of talk sounds like in our classrooms:

> You are getting ready to send out your political letters to some pretty powerful people all across the city and state, and you want them to pay attention to your words and ideas as they read your letters. Before you fold it, put it in the envelope, and send it off with a stamp, there are a few things that I want you to think about. When the person who receives your letter gets it, they won't only be taking in your words and ideas. They will also be judging you on the kind of writer you are. That means that they'll take in whether or not you have spelled words correctly and if you've used academic language. Words, ideas, and academic language—these are all the ways that writers express themselves, and these are all forms of power. But a reader might miss out on your powerful ideas just because you may have errors in academic language in your writing. I want you to be taken seriously, and you have worked so hard on these letters, that I know you want to be taken seriously too. I want the reader to take a look at your letter and think, "This is someone worth paying attention to." It's unfair that errors in academic language carry that much weight in our society, but I think you know that they do. The letters you have written show that you are not okay with all of the ways that people think in our society. Don't give people the opportunity to throw out or dismiss your letters because of your errors in academic language.

Raising the issue in this way, explicitly and honestly, empowers the students and gives real purpose to applying what they have learned about grammar and code-switching.

Annotated Lesson on Code-Switching

The first set of these lessons relates to one feature we noticed often in our students' writing: double negatives. Even though double negatives are fairly universal in oral language, this feature is a clear example of a language structure that does not align with academic language. We identified double negatives as our first rule because it was tangible—easy to identify and easy to modify for academic language.

Here is how the lesson goes (you'll notice that the sentences for correction require cumulative practice):

Distribute (about 1–2 minutes)

Give each student a copy of the handout (this includes the grammar rule, examples of the rule used correctly, and sentences for practice). Place a copy on an overhead transparency, or have the rule, examples, and sentences for practice visible on the board. Grammar Rule #15 is an example of a handout.

Connection (about 1–2 minutes)

"You remember my spiel on code-switching, the idea that you can switch between different dialects (ways of speaking) depending on your audience, and how crucial that is for you to learn in order to have all the options in the world open to you. We're going to start with double negatives because this is a clear way to start to see code-switching. You have been learning about negative numbers in math. Let's review what happens when negative numbers are multiplied. Take, for example, $-2 \times -2 = +4$. The two negatives cancel each other out and the answer becomes positive. If you have just one negative number and one positive number, $-2 \times 2 = -2$, the answer is negative. This same principle applies to double negatives in academic language. For example, if I were trying to tell my friend that I'm broke and I said, 'I don't have no money,' what I'd really be saying is 'I do have money,' because the negatives, the *don't* and the *no* cancel each other out and become a positive, just like in math. So instead I would say, 'I don't have any money.'"

GRAMMAR RULE #15: Double Negatives. Everyday language often uses double negatives, or two negative words in one sentence. (I *can't* find *nobody*.) Academic language includes only one negative word in a sentence. Usually, it's the second negative in the sentence that is to be changed. (I *can't* find *anybody*.)

Negative (−)	Positive (+)
nothing	anything
nowhere	anywhere
no/none	any
never	ever
nobody	anybody

Everyday Language

(*includes two negative words*)

He *didn't* do **nothing.**

Don't go **nowhere**!

I don't **got no** homework.

She *ain't* **never** home.

Academic Language

(*includes only one negative word*)

He *didn't* do **anything.**

Don't go **anywhere.**

I don't **have** any homework.

She *isn't* **ever** home.

Sentences for Practice: Change everyday language into academic language.

1. I didn't eat no delectable cake.

2. Don't belittle nobody! Its a toxic thing to do.

3. My mother couldn't find no pacifier's nowhere.

4. She don't got nothing to say because she's to timid.

Knowing how and when to use academic language instead of everyday language is called **code-switching.**

Teaching and Demonstration (about 3–4 minutes)

"Let's take a look at Rule #15: Double Negatives. Follow along as I read the rule to you. Everyday language often uses double negatives, or two negative words in one sentence, for example, 'I *can't* find *nobody*.' Academic language includes only one negative word in a sentence. Usually, it's the second negative in the sentence that is to be changed, for example, 'I *can't* find *anybody*.' Think back to $-2 \times -2 = +4$. If you say I *can't* (one negative) *find nobody* (another negative), then you technically end up saying the opposite: If you can't find nobody, then you can find somebody, which is why in academic language, people are uncomfortable with double negatives.

"Look at the table now to see which words are negative and which are positive. It's like opposites: *nowhere* is negative, *anywhere* is positive. Take a few seconds to read the rest of the table to yourself.

"Here's where it gets interesting, where we can see patterns in both everyday and in academic language around double negatives. 'He didn't do nothing' has a double negative in everyday language: *didn't* and *nothing*. In academic language, it's 'He didn't do *anything*.' *Didn't* is the only negative, and *anything* is positive. Take a minute to turn and talk with your partner about what you notice about the rest of the sentences showing the two patterns."

Active Engagement/Practice (about 5–8 minutes)

"Go ahead and practice with the four sentences. Remember that, as always, you're not only thinking about code-switching but also about other grammar rules we've learned so far." [*Note: In order to differentiate, you may choose to jot down the number of errors in the margin by each sentence for some students.*] Students may turn and talk with each other to share the ways they've fixed the sentences and to discuss what they're learning about double negatives in writing. After many students seem to be finished, you may want to go over the sentences together to share the understanding about double negatives.

Link to Ongoing Work (about 1 minute)

"Becoming aware of the patterns and knowing when and how to use which is what we mean when we talk about code-switching. Neither is right or wrong, both follow patterns, so it's all about context. When we are together in the classroom, it is an academic context. So, in our speech in here, we're going to go for academic language, meaning no double negatives. There won't be any punishment, obviously—just reminders. This is crucial practice for beginning to make code-switching something you do automatically.

"And, as we are writing essays now in writing workshop, and essays are an academic genre, academic language will be expected. Keep this in mind as you are writing today."

Evidence of Student Progress

Consider the following samples of student writing both before and after instruction around code-switching.

Before (bold italics show incorrect use of academic language patterns in writing)	After (bold italics show correct use of academic language patterns)
But then one day his mom had given me a gift for being a great tutor. So I *brang* the doll home and my older sister kept on teasing me saying he was my boyfriend. (Esther)	I first planned it out, what goes in what paragraph. After it was planned I *wrote* it in a letter form and Chantal checked it to give me suggestions. (Esther)
If the price goes too low, the *government don't like it*, but if the price gets too high, we don't like it. You need to know that riding the subway need to spend a lot of money . . . *He think* they should. . . . (Wai Ling)	*It* really *causes* so many problems. If *students fail* the state tests, *they will* get left back and *have* to repeat the grade. (Wai Ling)
I seen Joel walking down the street of Harlem . . . *Me and Joel been mad* at each other and he *don't* want to speak to me but *crying don't* make it better. (Roxanne)	Juror Three said, "I think *he's* guilty. *Does* anyone else?" . . . *She saw* the murder through the window of the last two cars on the train. (Roxanne)
I *did'nt* say *nothing*. (Devonti)	Just *'cause* I have no feelings for you *doesn't* mean *anything*. (Devonti)

Lessons on Code-Switching

As it was for inaudible errors, students investigating in their independent reading books continues to be an important extension for supporting understanding of everyday and academic language patterns. Some young adult books contain dialogue that is written using everyday language patterns. Some authors, like Sharon G. Flake, have written entire books using everyday language patterns. As students read with an awareness to these patterns, a chart for investigation could look like this:

Sentence or Phrase from the Text	Everyday or academic language? How do you know?	Why did the author do this?
"I didn't tell no lies!"	Everyday language because there is a double negative (*didn't* tell *no* lies).	To make it sound the way people actually talk.

Assuming you've taught Grammar Rule #15 as described early in this chapter, the next lesson is for review of this rule. This review could be done either in class later in the week or at home for homework.

GRAMMAR RULE #15 REVIEW: Academic language doesn't use double negatives.

> **Example:** She **doesn't** have **anything** to worry about.

Sentences for Practice: Change everyday language into academic language (and correct other grammar/spelling errors) in these sentences.

1. The scowl on my friend's face doesn't make no sense since I just gave her two piece's of delectable chocolate.

2. There isn't nothing nobody can do to stop that girl from dousing her brothers friend with water.

3. In Elvis essay he say's, "Homophobia hurts everyone, gay and straight." There ain't nothing as powerful as that.

We found that, in almost all of our students' writing, subject–verb agreement in academic language was a problem on many levels. Specifically, we saw students had difficulty differentiating between and correctly writing the three basic tenses (past, present, and future). Our students also demonstrated confusion using regular and irregular verbs.

While the challenges around verbs were overwhelming, we aimed to stay faithful to not burdening our students with lessons that would feel irrelevant to their development as powerful writers. Indeed, most grammar textbooks that we consulted to aid us in teaching these lessons offered seemingly endless units of tedious and monotonous fill-in-the-blank worksheets. They offered teaching students a wide range of new terms and rarely used rules related to the concept of subject–verb agreement. But we wanted to teach our students the rules and concepts that would address the most urgent aspects of their own writing. And, as the task of teaching verb conjugation became overwhelming, we did not hold our students to perfect mastery of every verb. Instead, we taught them that if they ever struggle with how to best conjugate a verb, then they can do what good writers do when in need: consult texts that can offer basic ideas and extensions of what we have offered here.

In tackling teaching subject–verb agreement, we found there was an order that seemed to make sense. We wanted students to have a general sense of what we meant when we said "subject–verb agreement," and introducing the sequence with pronouns, nouns, and regular verbs in the present tense was a good place to start. Next, we wanted the students to understand verb conjugation, and that many verbs in English are irregular. Given students' struggles with differentiating between present and past tense in their writing, we also developed lessons that addressed rules for writing specific tenses. Finally, we wanted students to learn that not all verb conjugations follow the same exact pattern, and introducing them to common irregular verb patterns was essential. The order of the following lessons reflect this thought process.

GRAMMAR RULE #16: Pronouns always agree with their verbs.

Examples:

	To talk	**To scream**	**To want**	**To wish**
I	talk	scream	want	wish
You	talk	scream	want	wish
We	talk	scream	want	wish
They/students	talk	scream	want	wish
She/he/it	talks	screams	wants	wishes

Sentences for Practice:

1. Helen smile as she greet students' everyday.

2. Ileana scowl whenever her nephew wakes her up in the middle of the night.

3. Many students complains that its difficult to read during Humanities when car alarm's go off outside, but Chantal just ignore the noise.

Developing Lessons on Code-Switching

GRAMMAR RULE #17: Indefinite pronouns must agree with their verbs in academic language. For regular verbs, when the pronoun is singular, the verb ends in **s**. When the pronoun is plural, the verb does not end in **s**.

Indefinite Pronouns

Singular			Plural	Singular or Plural
another	everyone	one	both	all
anybody	everything	other	few	any
anyone	much	somebody	many	more
anything	neither	someone	others	most
each	nobody	something	several	none
either	no one			some
everybody	nothing			

Examples:

- Everybody wants to go to Six Flags.

- Many people want to go outside for lunch.

- Some of the students wish they had no homework.

Sentences for Practice:

1. Many students notice that something smell good in the other room.

2. When Elisa say something to the class, almost everyone hear, but a few listens to they're friends instead.

3. When two students finishes there poetry anthologies their going to read their poem's to the class while others continues to write.

GRAMMAR RULE #18: Certain verbs must be conjugated differently than regular verbs.

	To be	**To do**	**To have**
I	am	do	have
You	are	do	have
We	are	do	have
They, students	are	do	have
She/he/it	is	does	has

Examples:

- Giselle does the same routine every Monday night—she watches *Prison Break* first, then she watches *24*.

- "We are very proud of you!" the parents exclaimed with fervor when their eighth-grade son achieved Honor Roll.

- You all have to work hard in school so you can earn a profitable income in the future.

Sentences for Practice:

1. Mark have a scowl on his face cause he picked up fourteen candy bar wrappers from the floor today.

2. "That don't make no sense!" the student's yelled when they learned they're school year would be extended to July 15.

3. Kathleen be growing delectable tomatos in the garden next to her brand knew apartment.

Note: Appendix D contains a chart of rules for words ending in *–ed*. Like the chart for plural spelling rules, this is meant to be a resource; you may want to review them or choose different rules to teach.

GRAMMAR RULE #19: To make the past tense with most regular verbs, add *–ed.*

If the verb ends in	How to make the past tense	Example
e	Drop the *e* and add *–ed*	Live—liv*ed*; date—dat*ed*
Consonant + *y*	Change *y* to *i*, then add *–ed*	Try—*tried*; cry—*cried*
One vowel + one consonant (*and one syllable or accent not on the first syllable*)	Double the consonant, then add *–ed*	Tap—ta*pped*; stab—sta*bbed*
Anything else	Add *–ed*	Boil—boil*ed*; fill—fill*ed*

Sentences for Practice:

1. The teacher immediately stoped talking to her student's because a mouse scurryed across the middle of the room.

2. The three childs had to be pacifyed after they broke out in tears because they're balloons sailled away.

3. We easily determind who the quack student was because he claped after the poem was read aloud while the other student's snaped.

4. The couple dated for only two weaks before they decided too get married.

GRAMMAR RULE #20: When writing in the *past tense*, some verbs are irregular.

	To be	**To do**	**To have**
I	was	did	had
You	were	did	had
We	were	did	had
They, teachers	were	did	had
He/she/it	was	did	had

Examples:

- *We were* all cheering when Ginessa finished her essay.

- *Mark was* about to give Jessica the new principal's book club book, but she already had it.

- *I didn't* want to tell my sister my students were making her a graduation card.

Sentences for Practice:

1. You was the only one who didnt do Ileanas homework.

2. We was emerging from the room when the girl cryed out in anguish.

3. Most of the student's was smitten with Beyonce, so they gaze at her picture for hours yesterday.

4. Those was the most delectable cookie's and nobody were ready to eat no more sugar.

5. The fireman remembered what he learn and so he stop, droped and rolled when he saw his pant's was on fire.

GRAMMAR RULE #21: Some irregular verbs in the past tense don't end in *–ed*. Their spelling is changed in other ways.

Present	Past
begin	began
break	broke
bring	brought
choose	chose
fall	fell
fly	flew
fell	felt
give	gave
go	went
grow	grew
know	knew

Present	Past
leave	left
lead	led
make	made
meet	met
pay	paid
run	ran
see	saw
speak	spoke
take	took
throw	threw
write	wrote

Examples:

- *Manny brought* his permission in on time.
- *The teachers chose* the students who were getting awards yesterday.
- *Lily spoke* in a whisper when she came in during independent reading.

Sentences for Practice:

1. Elisa payed for Chinese food the other night and she brung the leftover's in for lunch because the food be so delectable.

2. Yesterday he sit down and write four poems and feeled so happy because his poetry anthologies great.

3. I went against my intuition cause I knowed I shouldnt have told her my secrets; she breaked so many promise's in the past.

Grammar Quiz—Double Negatives and Indefinite Pronouns*

PART ONE

Directions: Edit the following paragraphs by circling the incorrect words and writing the correct spelling above the word. The first one has been underlined and changed as an example.

A New York Hospital is at the center of major fervor this week after two women
                                                          weren't
were implanted with the wrong embryos. They <u>wasn't</u> able to complete no pregnancies and had to have emergency operations to remove the embryoes. Everybody at the hospital be furious that the two doctors who are responsible for the implantes haven't received no punishment, while the president of the hospital has been suspended! Both of the doctors is happy they didn't get in no trouble.

    The womans intuition told them they was pregnant after the implant, and they was very happy because they was never able to make no babies on there own. They didnt have no idea that such a mistake could happen. Both is living in anguish. Many friends cames to there house to pacify them because their lifes are now in shambles.

    One nurse at the hospital said, "It don't make no sense that the people who performed the implant are still working here! No one know if they might do it again." Several agrees. They think if the doctors can't read no instructions, then they shouldn't have there jobs.

PART TWO

Directions: Choose ten pronouns from the box and write ten sentences that show correct subject–verb agreement.

This	That	You	All	Any	We	They	Both
Everything		Some			Few		
Somebody	Either	None			Many		
Anybody		Most			Several		
No one		More			Those		

1. _____

2. _____

3. _____

continued

* See Appendix E for the modified paragraphs for Part 1 of the Double Negatives and Indefinite Pronouns Quiz.

4. _____

5. _____

6. _____

7. _____

8. _____

9. _____

10. _____

GRAMMAR RULE #22: The action that a verb represents takes place at a certain point in time, or tense. Three important tenses are simple, continuous, and perfect. These tenses help us understand when the verb (the action) happens.

Examples:

	Present	**Past**
Simple	I **walk** to school.	I **walked** to school.
Continuous	I **am walking** to school right now.	I **was walking** to school when I saw you.
Perfect	I **have walked** to school since first grade. (the action began in the past, but is still happening)	I **had walked** to school until you started giving me a ride. (action began in the past and is done)

Sentences for Practice:

1. It didnt make no sense that she mad; she know better!

2. All the drawer's in his desk breaked so he call someone to fix it this morning.

3. Elisa have liked to eat candy since she a kid, but her dentist say for her to cut back on sweets.

Note: For Rule #23, it's important to remind students that when they use the continuous or perfect tense (use *had* or *have*), they need to use the past participle.

GRAMMAR RULE #23: Some verbs have irregular past participles. *Walked* is the past participle of *walk*; *eaten* (instead of *eated*) is the past participle of *eat*. (Regular: She has *walked*; Irregular: She has *eaten*).

Present	Past	Past Participle	Present	Past	Past Participle
am, be	was, were	been	know	knew	known
begin	began	begun	ride	rode	ridden
choose	chose	chosen	speak	spoke	spoken
do	did	done	steal	stole	stolen
drink	drank	drunk	swim	swam	swum
eat	ate	eaten	take	took	taken
fall	fell	fallen	tear	tore	torn
fly	flew	flown	throw	threw	thrown
give	gave	given	write	wrote	written

Examples:

- *Chantal had eaten* her lunch by 12:37.
- *The seventh graders had walked* quietly down the hall that morning.
- *The teachers had given* the vacation reading assignment two days before break.

Sentences for Practice:

1. He had wrote his cover letter two day's ahead of time.

2. He hasnt did his homework in three nights.

3. The class had just began doing they're independent reading when the fire alarm went off.

The following sentences for practice could be used as homework or for practice on another day.

Sentences for Practice:

1. Chantal has brung a delectable lunch to school every day for five years.

2. Kathleen scowled because her shirt had tore on the fence.

3. Elisa has flew in airplanes many time's in her life.

4. The boy was smitten. He had never saw such a beautiful person.

GRAMMAR RULE #24: There are some more important everyday and academic patterns to remember for code-switching.

Examples:

Everyday Language	Academic Language
That's *mines.*	That's *mine.*
I *been* told you.	I *already* told you.
I been there before.	*I have (I've) been* there before.

Sentences for Practice: Change everyday language into academic language (and correct other grammar/spelling errors) in these sentences.

1. Kathleen had took her dog to the park because she been they're yesterday and had fun.

2. The girls mother yelled, "I been told you to clean you're room six times!"

3. Even though he been saving for it, the mans income was to small to buy the new car.

4. The kid wasnt too timid to shout, "That candies mines!" when his friend grabed it away from him.

GRAMMAR RULE #25: Even more important everyday and academic patterns to remember for code-switching.

Examples:

Everyday Language	Academic Language
She *do* do that.	She *does* do that.
Why *you did* that?	Why *did you do* that?
What *this* do?	What *does this* do?
Where *you at*?	Where *are you*?

Sentences for Practice:

Using any of the everyday/academic patterns you've learned (the ones above, double negatives, etc.), write a dialogue of at least eight to ten lines that includes at last one speaker using academic language. (*Remember what you've learned about punctuating dialogue!*)

_____

_____

_____

_____

_____

_____

_____

_____

_____

_____

Grammar Quiz

PART ONE

Which One Is Correct for Academic Language?

1. The two main characters in *12 Angry Men* (was/were) Juror #3 and Juror #8.

2. The jurors deliberated (whether/weather) the boy was guilty.

3. Juror #11 corrected Juror #10 by saying, "He (doesn't/don't) speak good English."

4. The eighth-grade students (brought/brung) a lot of intensity to the play when they acted it out.

5. (Its/It's) a shame that (their/there) (weren't/wasn't) (no/any) movie producers watching the (classes/classes') performances.

Grammar Test Review: Sentences for Practice

Directions: Edit the following paragraphs by circling the incorrect words and writing the correct spelling above the word. (15 total)

Youve learned a lot about Elisa, Chantal and Kathleen since you started learning about grammar rules. You was amazed too learn that Kathleen have a dog! Some of you is astonished that Chantal brung her lunch every day for the passed five year's. And you also learned that Elisa dont eat no more candy cause her dentist told her two cut back. We hope you has enjoyed learning about you're teachers' this year.

Grammar Final Test

PART ONE (30 POINTS)

Directions: Edit the following paragraphs for academic language and correct grammar by circling incorrect words and writing the correct spelling above the word. The first one has been underlined and changed as an example. (25 total changes)

County Executive Passes Law Recognizing Gay Marriages

WHITE PLAINS, N.Y.—Gay marriage; <u>its</u> [it's] making headlines again. Westchester County have issued a law that makes it the first county in the state to recognize gay marriage's.

Andrew Spano reads the law Wednesday night at a meeting of gay groups and received a standing ovation. The law gived marryed gay couples the same privileges as heterosexual couples in Westchester County, just north of New York City. Some rights gay couples will receive are the right to by family passes to park's and the right two find emergency housing as a family.

"I dont see why people, just because their the same sex, shouldnt have no benefits," Spano says last Thursday. "People who is gay should not be belittled by the government. Its just knot fair."

The law does not mean that town's and villages in Westchester must say the marriages are legal and it does not help same-sex couples get state or federal privileges. It applies only too couples who were married in a state or country we're gay marriage is legally performed. Massachusetts is the only state in the U.S. where gay marriage be legal; Canada, Belgium, Spain and the Netherlands been legalized same-sex marriages.

In his speech, Spano said the New York law requires everyone to recognize a same-sex marriage that been done in another state, regardless of weather the marriage is permitted under New York law.

New York City have recognized legal gay marriages. Jordan Barr, a spokesman for Mayor Michael Bloomberg, said the City Council ratified legislation within the last two years. He added, "Mayor Bloomberg don't got no problem recognizing same-sex marriages."

PART TWO

Which One Is Correct for Academic Language? (20 points)

1. Some people believe that there (been/has been) progress since the Civil Rights Movement.

2. June 28th is the (students'/students) last day of school.

3. After the Voting (Rights/Right's) Act was passed, Joshua exclaimed, "Yeah! We don't have to take (no/any) more tests!"

4. After she (droped/dropped) her sister off at school, she (brought/brung) her books back to the library.

5. The average income for African Americans (is/are) still (to/too) low compared to the average income for whites.

6. Chantal glowered after she (seen/saw) the abysmal homework percentage of the day.

7. The student had (written/wrote) her cover letter before she had (came/come) to after-school.

8. (There/their) favorite TV show had (its/it's) final episode last night.

9. After segregation laws (was/were) declared unconstitutional, everybody (were/was) allowed to sit anywhere they wanted on city (busses/buses).

10. The bakery's (shelves/shelfs) (was/were) loaded with delectable cakes.

11. The mouse (scurried/scurryed) across the floor after Kathleen stepped on (it's/its) tail.

**Extra Credit: Make all the necessary corrections (2 points)

March is Womens' History Month. Several month's is dedicated to different group's of people. Witch is you're favorite?

_____

PART THREE (20 POINTS)

Directions: Write an essay about one of the topics below. You will be graded on your use of academic language and correct grammar.

Your eighth-grade experience	Cell phone/ iPod use in school	Same-sex marriage	Things that you regret

An Alternative Approach to Addressing Subject–Verb Agreement in Academic Language

You may notice that your students struggle with just a few verbs when it comes to subject–verb agreement in academic language. For instance, they may struggle only when choosing between *was* and *were* and *do* and *does*. As we've worked with teachers to fit this curriculum into their classrooms, many have decided to go this way when it comes to subject–verb agreement in academic language. If this is the case for your students, you may want to consider a contrastive analysis approach suggested by Rebecca Wheeler and Rachel Swords in *Code-Switching: Teaching Standard English in Urban Classrooms* (2006), and then follow our approach with sentences for practice. Their approach was instrumental in both helping us think through how to build off of what students already know about their own language patterns and in thinking about how to support students as they apply that knowledge to understanding language use in academic settings.

The contrastive analysis lesson begins with inquiry: the students discover the different language patterns for everyday and academic language, thus discovering the "rule." Students first compare and contrast what they notice about the patterns of a particular verb in everyday language and academic language sentences by examining a chart like the one below. Following this inquiry, they can make hypotheses about rules for agreement in both language patterns. You can guide them through this practice, noticing similar and different features in both languages. The sentences for practice assure that students will continue to build on previous lessons they have learned, and have a chance to practice their learning right away.

We have numbered the examples below as Rules #16A, #17A, and #18A, as though you were beginning your subject–verb agreement lessons with these instead of lessons with the same numbers earlier in this chapter. Of course, you may have different numbers anyway, depending on which lessons you decide to teach.

The first lesson is scripted below, to give you an idea of how the teaching of the lesson goes. Following the scripted lesson, we offer two other lessons that follow this same format.

Distribute (about 1–2 minutes)

Give each student a copy of the handout (this includes the grammar rule, a contrastive analysis chart, questions for them to answer about the chart, and sentences for practice). Place a copy on an overhead transparency, or have the rule, examples, and sentences for practice visible on the board. Grammar Rule #16A is an example of a handout.

GRAMMAR RULE #16A: Nouns and pronouns agree with their verbs. Study the chart below to see how *was* and *were* are used in everyday and academic patterns.

Everyday Language	Academic Language
I was reading.	I was reading.
The dog was reading.	The dog was reading.
She was reading.	She was reading.
Chantal was reading.	Chantal was reading.
We was reading.	We were reading.
You was reading.	You were reading.
They was reading.	They were reading.
The students was reading.	The students were reading.

1. What do you notice about the patterns for everyday language and academic language?

Sentences for Practice: Change everyday language into academic language (and correct other grammar/spelling errors) in these sentences.

1. The apartment was noisy because the resident's was having a party.

2. You was the first student to enter Giselles math class, and she was happy you was they're early.

3. We weren't going to tell you, but we was shopping for new book's yesterday because you told us there still wasn't enough books in our classrooms library.

Connection (about 1–2 minutes)

"We started thinking about code-switching, the idea that you can switch between different dialects (ways of speaking) depending on your audience, with double negatives. Another aspect important to code-switching is about subject–verb agreement, and there are a few particular verbs that I've noticed you struggling with."

Teaching and Demonstration (about 2–3 minutes)

"Let's take a look at Rule #16A: Nouns and pronouns agree with their verbs. Today we are going to study *was* and *were*. Take a look at the chart. On the left side are the patterns for everyday language, and on the right are the patterns for academic language. On the left under Everyday Language it says *I was reading,* and under Academic Language it says *I was reading* also. The patterns with the pronoun *I* are the same: you use *I was* in both everyday and academic language. You'll notice as you read, however, that there are some differences."

Active Engagement/Practice 1 (about 2–3 minutes)

"Study the chart, then write what you notice about everyday and academic language patterns for the question below the chart. You many want to talk with your partner as you study the chart and try to name what you notice." As students are studying the chart and answering the question, the teacher can circulate to see what the students are saying and writing. After most students are done, call them back together.

"Everybody seemed to be noticing the same things—that in everyday language, you might use *was* with all nouns and pronouns. But in academic language, you use *were* for *we, you, they,* and *the students.* So we could say that in academic language, you use *was* for singular nouns and pronouns, and *were* for plural nouns and pronouns. The pronoun *you* is an exception: you always use *were* with the pronoun *you.*"

Active Engagement/Practice 2 (about 5–8 minutes)

"Go ahead and practice with the three sentences. Remember that, as always, you're not only thinking about code-switching but also about other grammar rules we've learned so far." [*Note: In order to differentiate, you may choose to jot down the number of errors in the margin by each sentence for some students.*] Students may turn and talk with each other to share the ways they've fixed the sentences and to discuss what they're learning about *was* and *were* in writing. After many students seem to be finished, you will want to go over the sentences together.

Link to Ongoing Work (about 1 minute)

"Becoming aware of the patterns and knowing when and how to use which is what we mean when we talk about code-switching. Neither is right or wrong, both follow patterns, so it's all about context. Remember that when we are together in the classroom, it is an academic context. So, in our speech in here and in our essays that we are working on in writing workshop, we're going to go for academic language, meaning no double negatives and new attention to *was* and *were*."

Next are two more examples of this kind of lesson. These lessons address particular verbs we noticed our students grappling with. Remember that you can make these lessons specific to your students' needs. Turn to Wheeler and Swords' *Code-Switching* for more ideas on this as well.

GRAMMAR RULE #17A: Nouns and pronouns agree with their verbs. Study the chart below to see how *don't* and *doesn't* are used in everyday and academic language patterns.

Everyday Language	Academic Language
I don't care.	I don't care.
The dog don't care.	The dog doesn't care.
She don't care.	She doesn't care.
Elisa don't care.	Elisa doesn't care.
We don't care.	We don't care.
You don't care.	You don't care.
They don't care.	They don't care.
The students don't care.	Students don't care.

1. What do you notice about the patterns for *don't* and *doesn't* in everyday language and academic language?

Sentences for Practice: Change everyday language into academic language (and correct other grammar/spelling errors) in these sentences.

1. She don't have enough pages left in her notebook.

2. Our school doesn't tolerate messy hallway's: Mark don't ever walk by a piece of garbage on the floor without picking it up.

3. Chantal don't like waiting until after school to go to the gym, so she wake's up early so she can get their before school start's.

GRAMMAR RULE #18A: Nouns and pronouns agree with their verbs. Study the chart below to see how *be, am, are,* and *is* are used in everyday and academic language patterns.

Everyday Language	Academic Language
I be late.	I am late.
The dog be late.	The dog is late.
She be late.	She is late.
Elisa be late.	Elisa is late.
We be late.	We are late.
You be late.	You are late.
They be late.	They are late.
The students be late.	The students are late.

1. What do you notice about *be, is, am,* and *are* in everyday and academic language patterns?

Sentences for Practice: Change everyday language into academic language (and correct other grammar/spelling errors) in these sentences.

1. We be hoping that everybody comes to the dance on Friday.

2. Chantal say's she be staying after school today for homework help.

3. Your doing well in math and you're parent's be proud of that.

With this method, we are combining the contrastive analysis approach presented in Wheeler and Swords' book with the pattern of our lessons. Instead of learning the stated rule, students study the differences between everyday and academic language and discover the patterns for themselves before going on to practice those patterns. You can decide which approach to take to teaching subject–verb agreement with you students.

Developing Lessons on Code-Switching

6

Making It Stick Through Reinforcement and Assessment

Our curriculum of grammar lessons and exercises is but one of a number of practices that we employ to ensure that our students retain the information they have gained through our instruction. In addition to the forty-five minutes (three fifteen-minute lessons) a week of direct instruction, we also work to make sure everything we do and use in our classroom is conducive to ongoing practice and accountability with standard English usage. We rely on assessments to measure students' growth in specific grammar areas, extensions to lessons to support transfer from our grammar study to their own writing, and a variety of reinforcements that offer significant support to students, yet don't take up much time. In this chapter, we'll share our ideas for helping to make the teaching stick beyond lesson time, and we'll also include more extensive evidence of our students' progress in writing.

Making It Stick

Post All Rules in a Visible Area

We recommend that teachers find a place in their classrooms where they can post all the grammar rules and concepts they've taught (see Figure 6–1). It's important that these are highly visible and easy to read, and it's essential that teachers refer

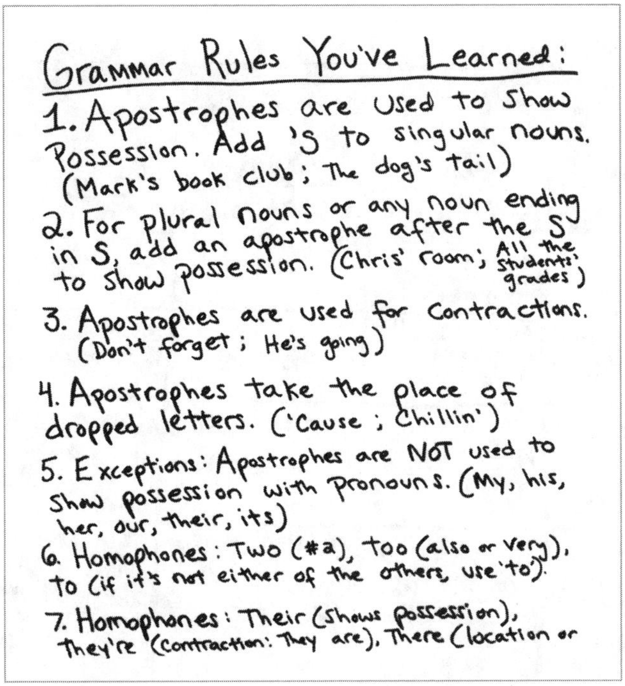

figure 6–1 Poster of Grammar Rules You've Learned

to these charts often so that students learn how to use them. Otherwise, the charts end up simply taking space rather than being a tool for students. To model using the charts, we would often point to the posters or walk over to them to show students how to find information. We would make verbal references to the charts as the need arises, such as during writing conferences, grammar lessons (as old rules are always folded into new ones in order to reinforce and provide opportunities for written and oral repetition), or any time a student asks a question or forgets a rule.

We titled these posters *Grammar Rules You've Learned*. We found it helpful to number the rules and concepts, to name them, and to include an example of usage. It helps if the poster is visually appealing and easy to navigate from students' desks, so we use markers to write different rules in different colors.

Some teachers choose to organize their posters by units of study rather than using the numbered list. That way, a teacher might have one poster for apostrophe rules, one poster for plural spelling rules, one poster of subject–verb agreement, and so on. Leona, a seventh-grade teacher, chose this method. One of her posters is shown in Figure 6–2.

What's the meaning of that APOSTROPHE?

Name	Rule	Example	Where does the apostrophe go?
Contraction	Apostrophe is used to show missing letters when 2 words are combined.	I can't go to the movies.	Usually where the missing letter(s) would go.
Missing or Dropped letter	To show a letter is missing (often in slang words)	We are chillin' on the steps.	Where the missing letter would be.
Possessive Singular (ownership)	To show one person owns something	This is Leona's classroom.	Add apostrophe then letter "s" at the end of the word.
Possessive Plural (ownership)	To show more than one person owns something.	ESCHS is the Students' school.	When word ends in letter "s" add apostrophe to end of word. * Some exceptions

figure 6–2 Leona's Poster of Apostrophe Rules

Use the Last Five Minutes of Class for Practice

You can devote the last five minutes of class for extra practice. These minutes can be planned into your schedule, such as committing to the last five minutes every Friday for grammar practice. If you can only teach one grammar lesson a week, we recommend spending a few moments at the end of class at least twice a week. In addition, there are some days when you may find that there are a few spare unplanned minutes at the end of class. You can put these minutes to use, with no additional preparation. Students can write their own sentence or two for a partner to correct. Ask them to intentionally include errors around the rules they have learned. Alternately, the teacher can write a sentence or two on the board for students to correct. It's always beneficial to have the students explain their corrections (either to a partner or to the class), consciously using the terminology. The students tend to enjoy this quick practice.

Annotate White Boards and Bulletin Boards

Annotating is an explicit and highly visible way to reinforce the rules. We annotated much of what we wrote that was visible to the students in class: the daily agendas on the white boards, homework assignments, and lessons on overhead projectors and bulletin boards. When doing a minilesson in any area of humanities and writing on the overhead projector, we'd say aloud why we were using that spelling of *they're*. If there were an apostrophe on the board, like "tonight's homework," we'd draw an arrow and label it "apostrophe for possession." Indeed, we became mildly obsessed (not a bad thing when teaching!) and consciously wrote on the board in styles that addressed particular rules we wanted to reinforce. Because many of our students were in the habit of adding an apostrophe whenever they wrote the letter *s*, plurals were erroneously punctuated. Thus, on bulletin boards, we'd label "8th Grade Editorials," draw an arrow and write "plural, no apostrophe!" Saturating the students by making them see, hear, and use the rules and language constantly and in varied ways played an important role in reinforcement (see Figure 6–3 for an example).

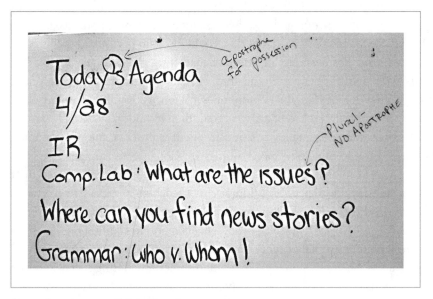

figure 6–3 Annotated White Board

Provide Opportunities for Students to Self- and Peer-Edit

One of the most critical and authentic places for reinforcement and connection is in the writing workshop. This is the time when the students are writing for authentic purposes and need to apply the rules they are learning—first as they edit (if they find places they've made errors) and then later as they write drafts. It's our goal that the grammar rules and concepts we teach are internalized and become habitual so that they apply them at all points in the writing cycle, not just when they are editing.

We held writing workshop four times a week. This time included a ten- to fifteen-minute minilesson on writing strategies particular to the genre we were studying, sustained writing time (during which the teacher conferred with individual or groups of writers), and a few minutes for share time when we reinforced or extended the lesson using student writing. We included the grammar and spelling rules into their editing procedures, updating expectations for self-editing as our students learned more. We made posters of the editing procedures and reviewed them toward the end of each sustained writing period.

One editing procedure suggested that students could whisper-read their writing following with a pen underneath each word. This way they are better able to see *and* hear any parts of their writing that need clarification or correction. We allowed our students to do this while working individually or they could try it with a partner. We also encouraged and then reminded students to practice self-editing at least twice for each piece, so that they could focus on particular aspects of grammar each time. For example, on the first read-through, they might look first for words with apostrophes or words that needed apostrophes. The second time through, they might look for homophones. When we found that many students were rushing through self-editing, we asked them to underline, say, all words with apostrophes, and write the kind of apostrophe it was above the word, reinforcing their use of the terminology and ensuring conscious, correct usage. One little tip: Having a jar of colored editing pencils to pass out at editing time infused the time with excitement and diligence. Middle school teachers are lucky in this way: It's amazing (and bizarre) how little things like sharpened, colored pencils can transform middle school students' buy-in and engagement. In addition, we had students edit their writing no matter what kind of writing they were doing for any of the content areas. So, if our students had written something during social studies, they were responsible for editing their content-area writing in the same way as they would edit during writing workshop. This kind of consistent editing is something we committed to daily, as we desperately wanted to turn editing into a habit. It is a step our students were not accustomed to doing regularly, yet it provided opportunities for independence and authentic application of the grammar rules they were learning. We found that regular self- or peer-editing can serve as a bridge enabling transfer between the stand-alone grammar lessons and our students' actual writing.

Teach Students to Investigate During Independent Reading

Investigation is a time when students notice the application of grammar rules in the books they read during independent reading. This idea came right from Mary Ehrenworth and Vicki Vinton's *The Power of Grammar* (2004). Diane Snowball and Faye Bolton's *Spelling K–8* (1999) also includes a wonderful chapter on inquiry work. Students use texts, preferably their independent reading books, as those tend to be the books in which students are most invested, to notice how authors use conventions and how the conventions affect meaning.

At East Side, all Humanities and English teachers begin each block with independent reading. During this time, students read books they've chosen for thirty minutes while the teacher conducts reading conferences with individuals. In our reading workshops, we begin with a whole-class minilesson a few days a week, and then we confer with individual or small groups of students. We also provide opportunities for students to respond to texts and write about strategies in their reader's notebooks, and they turn and talk about their reading at the end of the workshop. In their reader's notebooks, students take notes during minilessons, write about their books and use of strategies, practice reading strategies, and keep sticky notes after completion of a book. Turn and talk is a time when partners can share their thoughts about the books they read, the strategies they are using, ask questions, and notice and share authors' use of grammar rules in their books. The latter is what we will focus on here. Reader's notebooks and turn and talk are places to support students in the noticing of grammar rules in order to reinforce what they have learned. Before independent reading two days a week, we asked the students to call to mind the grammar rules they'd been learning (sometimes a specific one with which they were struggling), and to keep it in the backs of their minds or place a sticky note in their books when they saw that rule or symbol. Because we wanted students to get lost in the world of the book, we didn't want them to stop each time they noticed a rule. Rather, we wanted them reading with a consciousness of these things. Then, we would always give a minute or two at the end of reading time for students to flip back through the pages they read to find an example. At this point, they could turn and talk about their noticing. They could show the example and explain its use to their partners. Alternately, they could write this out in their reading notebooks on charts (see Figure 6–4). Looking for inspiration, we turned to Janet Angelillo's *A Fresh Approach to Teaching Punctuation* (2002) for ideas for charts.

We've included some samples from student reading notebooks. Here, students noticed how the authors of their independent reading books use apostrophes (these charts were completed during the time we were studying apostrophe use):

Example from Text	Symbol/Name	Why did the author do this?	Try it!
"Now we're your poster girls."	'/apostrophe	(Contraction) To make it sound like real speech	I decided I didn't want to go anywhere with him.
"Armpit's father worked in the daytime..." (p. 23)	'/apostrophe	To show that the father belongs to Armpit	My sister's pants are on the floor.

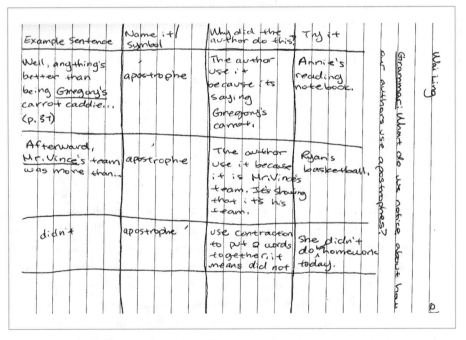

figure 6–4 Investigation Work in Wai Ling's Reader's Notebook

While we were studying homophones, we altered the chart. Here is what the students found in their independent reading books:

Sentence from Text	Word	What does the homophone mean?	Sounds like . . .
"I wouldn't have been watching."	wouldn't	would not	wood
"I've got some stuff to do too."	too	also	to

Using the charts, students copy the symbol (like an apostrophe), the rule they are noticing, the sentence from the book in which it appears, and then explain why and how it is used to create particular meaning.

While studying code-switching, we altered the chart once more. Here are examples of what Christopher found in his independent reading books:

Sentence from Text	Academic or Everyday?	How do you know? Why did the author choose this?
• "You too scared"	• everyday	• She wrote "You too scared," (instead of "You are too scared" which would be academic) to make it sound the real way the character talks.
• "We were coming from English"	• academic	• We *were* is academic, we *was* is everyday

Using this chart, Christopher did the following: He copied a sentence or phrase from his book; identified whether the sentence was in academic or everyday language; he described why the author made the choice to write in the language used; and contemplated how he knew what kind of language was being used.

We found it to be important to model this activity on an overhead projector or board before asking the students to do it. This is one of those areas that we assumed would happen automatically for students. We thought that if they were reading every day, they would absorb the rules from their reading. It just didn't turn out to be true for most of our students. We've both experienced lightbulbs going off in students' heads during these noticing activities. Elisa never will forget a moment in her class when during an inquiry on punctuating dialogue, Jessica, one of the most avid readers she has ever taught, said, "Oh! I've never noticed that before!" after realizing how the author of the book she was reading punctuated dialogue. This noticing work is exciting, too, when the students are studying code-switching, as so many young adult novels have characters whose speech patterns differ from academic English. This kind of reinforcement is crucial because they are actively noticing how these rules are used by published writers. This provides another context in which to see the rules, which offers additional and crucial reinforcement. Here is a sample minilesson plan for this work:

- *Connection:* When you are learning a new sport, you can learn the rules of the game, but they don't mean much until you see professionals put those rules to use and try using those rules out for yourself. The same goes for the rules around using apostrophes that we've been studying.
- *Teaching Point:* We are going to chart words that have apostrophes by investigating over the next week to see how published authors use them.
- *Demonstration:* "Take a look at the first two paragraphs from *Pink and Say*." [*Note:* You would use a part of any text that was already familiar to the class, and that had some clear examples of what you want them to notice. A read-aloud you'd done at some point would be perfect. That way, they are not distracted by the content of the story and can focus on apostrophe use, or whatever you are beginning to study. In this case, after combing through the read-alouds we'd done, we saw that *Pink and Say* uses apostrophes in several ways in a short length of text, so it was perfect.] "We read this a couple of weeks ago, and this time I want you notice the apostrophe use. Watch me as I start: I'll run my finger under the words, looking for apostrophes. Here's one! Once I've found one, I'll jot it down on this chart in my reader's notebook."

Word/Phrase	Symbol/Name	What I Think It Means	Try it!
I'd been	'/apostrophe for contraction	I had	He'd been late every day.

- *Active Engagement:* "Can you continue this? Quickly draw the chart. Make sure to have the chart take up a full page in your reader's notebooks, as you'll be adding to it several times over the next two weeks. Take sixty seconds to do that now. Okay: I'll give you four minutes to get as many examples into the chart as you can. Everybody should be able to get four examples, some of you might get even more." [This adds a challenge that resonates with many students.]

- *Link:* "As you are reading this week, along with all of the other work you do as readers, I want you to notice words that have apostrophes. You'll be charting them to see what you can determine about the rules for using them. I'll give you a few minutes at the end of independent reading to flip back through the pages you read and chart the words with apostrophes. I'm going to ask you *not* to stop and chart as you read, as that will interrupt your reading and interfere with your enjoyment and comprehension of reading— but keeping it in mind as you read will help you learn the rules. You can put a sticky note in the margin next to words with apostrophes if you like, but don't interrupt your reading to chart them."

- After independent reading time two to three times a week, give the students four to five minutes to flip back through the pages they read and chart examples of the rules they are studying. We say something like this: "Find a good place to stop and record on your reading record. Now flip back through the pages you read today, looking for words with apostrophes. I do this by just looking out for the apostrophe like we did during the minilesson. Some of you marked words with sticky notes, and some of you will go back and find examples now. Take four minutes to do that now. Everyone should find at least two examples, some of you will find more. Turn and talk with your partner about some of the words you found today."

This investigative part is crucial to the stickiness of the rules. You only have to do this minilesson one time per unit, and then students can continue collecting and adding to their charts after independent reading.

Reinforce Learning in Content-Area Classrooms

We want to ensure the practice of academic language in our classrooms. Yet one of the primary goals of teaching this grammar curriculum is for our students to understand how and when to use the rules of academic language in all academic settings. That means that their proficiency in academic language need not be limited to what they do only in Humanities. Instead, students should hold themselves accountable for what they learn about grammar when they write math problems, science labs, and history research papers. To do this, students can use their writing notebooks, in which the rules they have learned are taped, as a reference for all of their written work. If possible, posting the rules in other content-area teachers' classrooms pushes the reinforcement further. We each decided on a poster to be in charge of: Chantal was responsible for keeping the poster in science up to date, and Elisa was responsible for keeping the math teacher's poster current. That way, when the students were writing in their other classes they were encouraged to apply and transfer their learning. It also provided extra accountability, as they were being held accountable every time they wrote, no matter where they were or what subject they were studying.

Students should learn to incorporate their knowledge of academic language as they continue to develop into powerful writers in high school as well. Students need to be able to retain their knowledge of academic language as they get older. To encourage this, we collaborate with the high school teachers at our school and communicate to them our students' strengths with academic language and areas where they might need additional support. We pass along the rules to the teachers in the next grade to post in their rooms. As eighth-grade teachers, we chose the rules that students needed the most reminding on, typed those up, and passed on to the ninth-grade humanities teachers to post as "Grammar Rules You Learned Last Year" (see Figure 6–5).

GRAMMAR RULES YOU LEARNED LAST YEAR:

1. Apostrophes are used to show possession. If the noun is singular, add **'s**. (Examples: Mark**'s** office; the dog**'s** tail; The girl**'s** hair)

2. For plural nouns or any noun ending in **s**, just add the apostrophe after the **s**. (Examples: The student**s'** report cards; the ninth grader**s'** bake sale; He got the clas**s'** attention)

3. Apostrophes are used for contractions. They take the place of dropped letters when combining two words. (Examples: *don't*; *can't*; *didn't*)

HOMOPHONES YOU LEARNED:

1. **There** (place—over there); **they're** (they are); **their** (their books—pronoun possession)

2. **It's** (it is); **its** (its tail—pronoun possession)

3. **Two** (the #2); **too** (also, very); **to** (all other uses)

figure 6–5 List Passed on to Ninth-Grade Teacher

Similarly, the seventh-grade teachers passed their list to us. This way, students are reminded and held accountable for what they learned the year before. Students can begin to build on what they know, their knowledge of academic language can become more sophisticated, and they can become more adept at making choices of language in their writing.

It is through all of these methods that reinforcements and connections are made, bridging the gap between isolated lessons and usage in context. Incorporating all of them, as many as you can, or coming up with your own will only serve to enhance their learning. The more you can do consistently the better. It is the combination of these methods that helps the students remember, practice, observe, and finally habituate the grammar lessons, allowing them to learn new rules, break old writing habits, and form new ones.

Assessment

Ultimately, we want our students to be able to use what they have learned about mechanics and have the power to independently apply it to brand-new writing situations. Therefore, we intend to hold students to what they learn about Standard Written English by engaging in frequent practice throughout the week on a particular area of grammar. In order to deepen students' understanding of what they learn, we also incorporate both formative and summative assessments related to what students are working on. Mary Ehrenworth and Vicki Vinton's *The Power of Grammar* (2004) helped us understand that there are different levels of mastery of mechanics in writing. Whereas students assume a superficial acquisition of some writing strategies as they notice or edit their writing, they have a deeper sense of what they learn if they are doing it while they revise, draft, or write more informal pieces. Thus our assessments aren't about us and our teaching. Instead, our assessments aim to help students think about what they are learning, their level of mastery, and where they need extra support.

Additionally, our method of planning units backward through Understanding by Design (UbD) made us accountable to everything, big and small, that we committed to teaching during the span of each unit. So at the end of any given unit, during our planning meetings, we could always revisit our UbD sheets, along with student products from that unit, to truly assess what students learned and areas where we continued to see weaknesses. This process let us determine what areas we might need to continue to work on in upcoming units. Through our planning, we considered both formative and summative assessments for our students' learning so that we could think about daily opportunities for us to monitor our students' progress and also gain a sense of what they learned at the end of each unit.

Both *The Power of Grammar* (2004) and our planning methods are critical in our grammar work because these ideas allow us to articulate exactly which areas of grammar we intend to teach during a unit. Because students learn grammar in the context of their writing workshop units, we know that the areas of grammar we choose to include have to represent a manageable list, perhaps only three or four areas in a unit. We also are able to prepare our UbD sheets to reflect a cumulative understanding of the areas of grammar that students will learn in a semester: the aim is for the strategies of one unit to become the foundation for acquiring the strategies of the next unit. Indeed, some areas of grammar may be repeated from one unit to the next to send the message that mastery and retention, particularly in grammar, takes practice, practice, practice.

Quizzes and Tests

In following the features of the grammar curriculum, we intended for our assessments to seem as authentic as possible, and mirror the kinds of work that students would normally practice with their writing. We chose to include two parts on our quizzes, one in which students continue to practice editing, and one in which students have to write a paragraph or more on demand. The first part of the quiz is identical to what students do each time they learn a new rule: there are a handful of sentences that feature errors common in our students' work and they must use their editing skills to correct them. Because we have a population of students with different learning skills, we also provide modified quizzes to some of our students. Our aim is not to trick students or punish them, but again, to encourage them to deepen their understanding of what they are learning. Our modified quizzes tell students how many errors they will find in each sentence. Indeed, we still hold our students accountable for what they are learning, but offer them support when we deem it necessary.

In the second part of a quiz, we ask students to demonstrate their knowledge of the most recent areas of grammar they have learned thus far and use them in a paragraph that they write about a subject of their choice. We group the areas of grammar together for one quiz. For example, everything that the students have learned about apostrophes appears in one quiz. Synthesizing this information is more like what they would be asked to do in a real writing situation—employ multiple strategies at one time. The grammar test, which looks similar to the quizzes, is a more comprehensive, summative measure of how well students are able to do this.

Rubrics

We also assess students at the end of each major area of grammar instruction. In order to make assessment of grammar knowledge a presence in writing workshop, we include the topics they have learned in grammar on each rubric under a category marked *Conventions*. We make this assessment cumulative so that each rubric includes the topics of grammar that students have learned since the beginning of the year. Conventions count usually about 10 to 15 percent of the final grade for each genre. In order for students to get full credit on their rubric, their correct use of academic language should not just appear on final drafts. Rather, we want to see that students have been able to incorporate what they've learned about academic language throughout all stages of the writing cycle. Editing a final draft and making corrections there shows partial understanding of academic language, for which students will receive partial credit. Yet to earn full credit, students need to use what they learn about academic language in all academic writing, even the unpolished pieces (Ehrenworth and Vinton 2004). This demonstrates that students are taking ownership of using academic language and shows the ability to apply what they have learned in grammar to a brand-new situation (Wiggins and McTighe 2005).

We used the rubrics not only for final, summative assessment at the end of each unit but also as formative assessment. After drafting or revising, we would collect the students' pieces and assess them using the rubric. That way, students were expected to make further revisions according to the rubric, and see how they were doing with conventions (as well as in other areas on the rubric) during the writing process (see Figure 6–6).

Students as Teachers

Teaching others is one of the best ways to demonstrate learning and make knowledge deeper and more firmly implanted in the mind. Knowing this, we decided that one of the assessments for grammar would be for students to make an annotated poster that names, defines, and shows a particular rule being used correctly. At East Side, we end each semester with portfolio roundtables, where students present and defend their learning to other students, outside guests, family members, and teachers (see Figure 6–7). Students create and present one of these posters during this time. However, having roundtables is not a requisite factor to creating and presenting these posters. Students can then present these posters to classmates or younger students. It is a way for them to formalize and take ownership over their learning, and to articulate and transfer that knowledge to others.

Name ___Christopher___   Block ___

How Do You Write A Powerful Essay?

	Exceeds Standard (*meets all standards and...*)	Meets Standard	Approaching Standard	Unsatisfactory
Genre/ Structure	• Included extra body paragraphs • Explored the other point of view 31	Wrote a powerful editorial that included: • Introduction (✓lead, ___problem/topic, ___important information, ✓thesis statement) • At least 3 body paragraphs (✓assertion, ✓evidence and details, ✓concluding sentence) • Conclusion (✓other point of view, ✓restated thesis, ✓inspiring last sentence) 25	*(21 circled)*	18
Content/ Subject	Gathered evidence extensively 15	✓Showed knowledge of the topic ✓Used appropriate evidence to persuade the reader ✓Included appropriate transition words ✓Included quotations effectively *(circled)*	*(10 circled)* 9	6
Process/Effort	Took risks and revised extensively and independently 23	✓Followed the Writing Cycle ✓Notebook (___Has up-to-date table of contents, ✓Evidence of using strategies taught in class) ✓Participation in class (used class time productively and was a productive writing partner) ✓Turned in drafts on time *(19 circled)*	16	13
Conventions	Worked on editing, spelling, and conventions throughout writing process. 19	✓Corrected spelling of circled words, especially ___ e/ie words, ✓apostrophes, ___ plural nouns, and *proper noun not capitalized* homophones ✓Used correct punctuation for beginnings and ends of *capitalized* sentences and evidence ✓Followed procedures for final draft ✓Recopied/retyped draft with teacher corrections 16	*(12 circled)* *(8 circled)*	9
Voice	Outstanding use of sophisticated and academic language 12	✓Uses academic language ✓Shows emotion and investment in topic ✓Opinion is strong and clear 10	7	4

Final Grade: 70 C-

Comments:

figure 6–6 Rubric for the Essay Writing Unit

figure 6–7 A Student Presenting at Roundtables

The idea here is that we are asking students not only to learn new things but to make that learning habitual. Again, it is important to remember that we are asking them to think about how to communicate appropriately to their audience, to learn something new, and to have a lasting understanding of the tools they have learned through this curriculum.

These multiple reinforcements play a crucial role in holding students accountable for what they learn.

Success of the Curriculum: Evidence of Our Students' Progress

As the year progressed, while our students grew as powerful writers during writing workshop, they grew increasingly more capable of making informed choices about when and how to apply grammar rules and academic language to their writing. We observed them debating the placement of apostrophes with their writing partners, defending their choices to use everyday language in poems about their personal lives, and taking more risks in expressing their voices on paper. We think it is powerful to examine their work side by side to see their growth. The examples here show the progress that two students, Chris and Kenya, made in their writing between the fall and spring of their eighth-grade year (Figures 6–8 through 6–11).

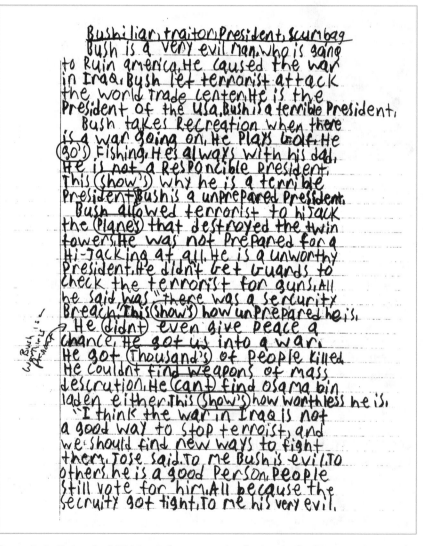

figure 6–8 Christopher's Writing Before Instruction (a First Draft of a Persuasive Essay)

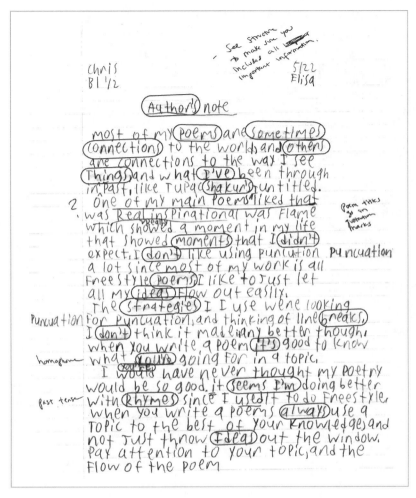

figure 6–9 Christopher's Writing in the Spring, After Instruction (a Draft of an Author's Note for His Poetry Anthology)

Circled words or words in bold italics show errors before instruction and then growth after instruction.

In the fall of eighth grade, Roxanne mixed everyday language and academic language, unable yet to consciously consider how and when to code-switch. By the spring, she had learned to make conscious choices in her writing, based on audience and voice, around code-switching (see Figures 6–12 through 6–14).

One of the scariest parts of being a teacher is letting go. While we invested so much into teaching this curriculum, and saw evidence of our students' progress in

Too many negative and positive feelings at once, not feeling wanted, lied to, used, manipulated, and not trusted. I hated feeling like a criminal in my home and *friends* house. I wanted out and I wanted it now!

One night when I came home after school, I walked across East Houston Street and thought *whats gonna* happen to me. Oohh I knew I should have left earlier, but I was having fun. Okay Okay I'll just speed walk so I *wont* be *extremly* late but I know it *wont* make a difference. The intercom at last now to dial: 0117.

"Who" my mother answered sounding as if she couldn't *belive* some one was calling.

"Open" I replied pretending to not realize how she spoke. My mother *did'nt* let me in I guess because this was a constant issue. So I went back to where I was which was my *friends* house.

"What happened?" My friend questioned.

"My mother got mad and *aint* let me in. Is it alright if I—"

"Kenya?! Of course," she cut me off.

figure 6–10 Kenya's Draft of a Personal Narrative Before Instruction

You, You, You

You *don't* treat me with respect
You always question who
I'm on the phone with
You make me think you *don't* want
to be with me
You were the one who broke up with me

figure 6–11 Kenya's Draft in the Spring, After Instruction (a Poem)

just a few months, we wondered if they would continue to hold on to what they learned about grammar and academic language beyond our classrooms. But when our students graduated from the eighth grade and entered East Side's high school, we still had the opportunity to see evidence of their growth as writers who understand the rules of grammar and of academic language during portfolio roundtables. Two years later, when Elisa read one of her former student's writing, she realized that this curriculum mattered to Rynetta and it had become an integral part of who she was as a writer (see Figures 6–15 through 6–17).

He Drives Me Crazy!

Have you even been in love, and it feels just so perfect? Well I have and **heres** my story. **I meet** Joel about 4 months ago and **been going** out for 3 months. **I seen** Joel walking down the street of Harlem. Joel had the red and white tens on his feet with a red and white tee on. At that moment I felt very excited because Joel was coming to see me and that **ment** something to me that he was real not just some kid fronting on me. A lot of people hated on me and Joel but we just Ignored it. I loved every minute me and Joel spent together. I remember that sweet smell that Joel always had on him, even though Joel never told me what it was. I love it when Joel walks and his chain makes that sound I really **cant** expain it but that I found spec'el to me. **Me and Joel been mad** at each other and He **don't** want to speak to me but crying **don't** make it better. Me crying at night and being so depressed **wont** make him come back. All I want to do is make him notice that he lost a big part of me and will never have it back. I grew so much since then and realized that people will come and go but will always be in my heart. People **dont** always stay together. We all have to grow apart but will always be in each **others** hearts.

figure 6–12 Roxanne's Writing Before Instruction (a Page from Her Writer's Notebook)

Gossip Folks

I can't even believe
you would try to hurt me

Just 'cause
I have no feelings for you
doesn't mean anything

I feel bad for you
I can't believe I loved you
after all we been through
together

You gonna go
and tell my man
that I was playin' him

I'm a ride or die chick
Ain't nothing gonna change that
'cause I love my baby

But
hataz will be hataz no matter
what!

figure 6–13 Roxanne's Writing After Instruction (Showing How Writers Can Choose Everyday Language in Poetry)

We attribute Rynetta's continuing progress to more than the individual components of our curriculum: the fifteen-minute lessons, or just the investigation work, or just annotated posters, or any single writing conference. We believe instead, all these parts, working together, enabled the change. The trajectory of Rynetta's, Kenya's, Chris', and all of our students' writing is a testament, we think, to the success of the overall curriculum.

East Side Community High School
C/O Elisa Zonana
420 East 12th street
New York, New York 10009
February 16, 2006

Ms. Oprah Winfrey
HARPO productions
P.O. Box 909715
Chicago, IL 60607

Dear Ms. Oprah Winfrey:

Hello. How are you doing today? Well, I'm doing fine. I am writing you today to inform
you about a special person in my life and who has helped me though it all. My name is Roxanne Dominguez. I am 13 years old and attend East Side Community High School.
I am also writing you for help.

My grandmother's name is Maria Velez. She's about 60 years old. She works as a computer technician and does not get paid very much. I love my grandmother dearly and would do anything for her. She took care of me for basically my whole life. My mother said that she "couldn't" take care of me so I was off to live with my grandmother. My grandmother has sacrificed a lot for me, once she used the rent money to buy me a pair of sneakers (which I really didn't need but wanted them so bad). She has been my role model for as long as I can remember. I have always tried to be like her. I have learned many things from her. She is growing old now, as I am. My grandmother is unable to work very long hours each day.

She has nowhere to live now and my mother is raising two little ones and me and my sister Pebbles. My stepsister is in college so my mother really does not need to worry about her so much. We only have two bedrooms and there is not much room. And there are 6 people living there already. My house is small but clean and a place where my grandmother can live her life safe. My grandmother is living with us and I really don't have a problem with it it's just to many of us in one small apartment.

I would love it if you could help me try to find her a home where she could be happy and maybe close to where I live. I would love to give back the love she has given me. I would love it if you could help my grandmother Maria find and me a home for her.

Thank you for taking the time out of your hectic schedule and I can't wait to read what you have written back and what you think about my letter.

Sincerely Yours,

Roxanne Dominguez
Roxanne Dominguez

figure 6–14 Roxanne's Writing After Instruction (Showing How Writers Use Academic Language in Business Letters)

THE GRAMMAR CURRICULUM

Dear Reader:

If you were in a *humanitie's* class do you think that you would like the class and pass it? Hello my name is Rynetta. I attend East Side Community High School. I am in 8th grade. I am supposed to be in 10th grade this year but it's a long story. My birthday is on February 11th so I'm about to be 16. The purpose of this letter is to inform *reader's* about what the class learned in *humanitie's* this year.

In Independent Reading this year we learned how to be powerful *reader's*. To be a powerful reader you have to keep a reading record of the *book's* that you read throughout the year. Also you have to keep another record *wich* is a list of *book's* that you have completed this year because that *keep's* you organized. Also to succeed in reading you need post-it *note's*. You also need to read a lot. In *humanitie's* we have to read every day and every night. For the homework and classwork. This year so far I have completed 21 *book's*. One of my favorite *book's* is Kicked Out by Beth Goobie.

<u>Kicked Out</u> is about a girl named Diane that *get's* kicked out of her house because she *always's come* home late. Then she *move's* out of her house because she *always's* come home late and her *parent's* complain so she *move's* in with her brother. She had a better life. Then she moved back to her real house and started to get along with her mom. My other favorite book is the book called <u>Is He a Girl?</u> by Louis Saachar. This book is about a boy that *meet's* a girl in class . . .

figure 6–15 Rynetta's Writing Before Instructions (a Draft of a Cover Letter for Roundtables)

One of my political *letters* that I wrote was a letter to the chancellor. It was talking about how *it's* not fair that if you are often late to school you *can't* get a job because it *depends* on your attendance record and it *shouldn't*. The way to become a powerful or political writer is 1) write out evidence *paragraphs* 2) have background information about what you are trying to get through to people 3) have a concluding sentence and a rough draft before you do the final letter. The way that I made *revisions* from my rough draft to my final draft is by writing the zip code and the address. Also because since I was typing so fast I realized that I misspelled some *words*. Then I did it over and spelled them correctly.

The thing that I learned about grammar is that the *apostrophes* in the *words* are used for *contractions*. Also they take the place of dropped letters when you combine 2 words. Example: *It's* raining today so *they're* staying inside. That is the correct way of doing it but we had to correct the *sentences* that *don't* have *apostrophes* and everything else that is it supposed to have.

figure 6–16 Rynetta's Cover Letter in the Spring, After Instruction

Dear Reader:

Hi. My name is Rynetta. I prefer to be called Hazel. I attend East Side Community High School. I am in 10th grade, and for English class I am in *Safiya's* class. This letter that I'm writing is about the *things I've* learned from English this semester. I hope you enjoy it. So basically, in this semester of English I learned a lot of *topics*, but as of right now I'm going to tell you *readers* about specific *topics*.

The topic that I learned was inner thinking. The piece of work that I have to show you *readers* that has inner thinking in it is the piece that I wrote about my job at Wendy's. The part of my writing that I wrote inner thinking is when I say, "Then the girl Lakisha on my job looked at me, then started sucking her teeth and having an attitude. I was just thinking to myself and saying to myself: if this girl wants to keep having an attitude she *needs* to stop."

Basically this piece of writing *talks* about how Lakisha from my job had caught her attitude with me, but basically the main topic that this piece is focusing on is how people choose to have *attitudes* at work in general.

figure 6–17 Rynetta's Cover Letter Two Years Later

Name: _____   Grade: _____   Subject: _____   Unit: _____

What are they getting?	What are they struggling with?
Implications for Teaching: (Consider what lessons you need to teach; should they be whole-class, minilessons, or small-group instruction?)	

Name: _____ Grade: _____ Subject: _____ Unit: _____

✓+ = Mastery ✓ = Basic Understanding ✓– = Approaching X = Not Understanding

Skill/Concept/ Strategy ⬆										Implications for Teaching (Consider what lessons you need to teach or change; should they be whole-class, minilessons, or small-group instruction?)
Student Names										

Name: _____ Grade: _____ Subject: _____ Unit: _____

What can our students' writing tell us?

What do you notice? (You can include content, genre/structure, theme, use/misuse of strategies, voice, use/misuse of conventions, vocabulary, organization, emotional impact . . . anything!)

What are some things we need to teach? (According to above observations, what lessons do you need to teach in this unit or the next unit? How will a lesson or lessons change or be different this year? What do you want to keep an eye out for as you continue to look at their work?)

APPENDIX B *Understanding by Design Framework*

Unit Title: Essay   **Course:** Eighth-Grade Humanities, Writing Workshop

S T A G E 1 D E S I R E D R E S U L T S

Big Ideas and Understandings:

- How to write a five-paragraph essay, including an introduction, body, and conclusion.
- Plan and draft an essay (apply writing cycle to essay).
- How to use evidence to support thesis.
- Understand different purposes and types of essays.
- Be able to write an essay in one sitting.

Essential Questions:

- How do you write a powerful essay?
- How do you support your thesis with evidence?

Essential Skills and Content:

Students will be able to . . .

- Write and develop a thesis statement.
- Apply writing cycle increasingly independently.
- Write an essay in one sitting.
- Write with attention to audience (how to persuade a reader).
- Include evidence and supporting details.
- Include quotations (punctuated correctly) in body paragraphs.

Students will know/understand . . .

- Transition words (*therefore, thus, in conclusion*)
- Paragraph and essay structure
- What it means to be an effective writing partner
- What language is appropriate for each genre
- How to write an effective ELA essay (essays from articles, stories, theme based, and using evidence from one or two different texts)

Vocabulary:

Thesis
Evidence
Editorial
Assertion (topic sentences)
Detail and concluding sentences

Grammar:

Apostrophe
Plural nouns
Homophones
Paragraph

Also accountable for: personal spelling list, *ie/ei* words, beginning and ending punctuation, punctuation evidence

Assessments:

(How will the students demonstrate that they learned the essential skills, content, and understandings?)

- Two editorial exhibitions (50% of total grade) with a rubric
- Two examples of timed, text-based essays (50% of total grade) with the ELA rubric

Feedback, Coaching, and Use of Data to Inform Instruction:

(How will information from assessments result in more student learning?)

- Daily writing conferences (each student, twice a week)
- Looking at students' notebooks and drafts during planning meetings
- Small-group support during writing workshop
- Assess student drafts using rubric (students make revisions based on feedback)

Learning Activities and Instructional Approaches:

(What will equip the students in learning and demonstrating the essential skills, content, and understandings?)

- What issues do teens have? (brainstorm and freewrite)
- Freewrites
- What are the features of editorials? (persuasiveness)
- How do you develop a thesis statement and plan an essay?
- How do you plan body paragraphs and develop assertions?
- How do you gather evidence and what types of evidence are there?
- How do you plan your body paragraphs?

(Additional lesson objectives are not provided here.)

Timeline:
November 2 to January 15
Editorials: November 2 to first week of December
ELA essays: second week of December to January 15

Resources and Mentor Texts:
Tiger's Eye (student literary magazine)
TC Reading and Writing Project materials
Atwell's *Lessons That Change Writers*

Unit Title: Essay   **Course:** Eighth-Grade Humanities, Writing Workshop

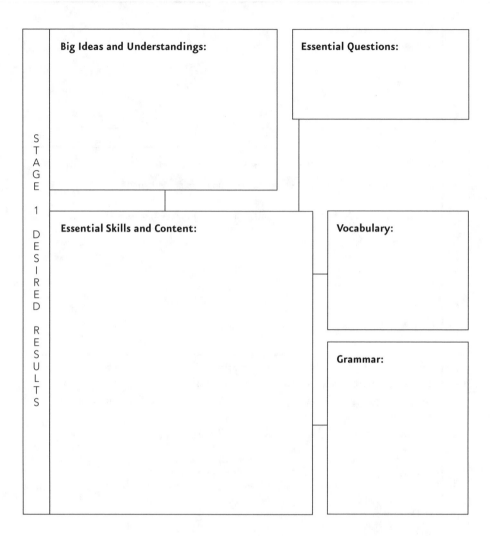

STAGE 1 DESIRED RESULTS

Big Ideas and Understandings:

Essential Questions:

Essential Skills and Content:

Vocabulary:

Grammar:

STAGE 2 ASSESSMENT AND EVIDENCE

Assessments:

Feedback, Coaching, and Use of Data to Inform Instruction:

STAGE 3 INSTRUCTION

Learning Activities and Instructional Approaches:

Timeline:

Resources and Mentor Texts:

GRAMMAR RULE:

Examples:

●

●

●

Sentences for Practice:

1.

2.

3.

GRAMMAR RULE:

Examples:

●

●

●

Sentences for Practice:

1.

2.

3.

APPENDIX D *Two Rules for Teacher Reference*

RULES FOR MAKING NOUNS PLURAL

Rules	Just add -s	When noun ends in consonant + y, change y to i and add –es	When noun ends in vowel + y, just add –s	When noun ends in consonant + o, add –es	If noun ends in vowel + o, just add –s	If noun ends in f, fe, or lf and has an f sound, just add –s	If noun ends in f, fe, or lf and plural has a v sound, change the f to v and add –es	Irregular
Words/Examples	dog/dogs	baby/babies	key/keys	tornado/tornadoes	radio/radios	chief/chiefs	wife/wives	foot/feet

Rules	When noun ends in ch, add –es	When noun ends in x, add –es	When noun ends in sh, add –es	When noun ends in s or ss, add –es
Words/Examples	beach/beaches	box/boxes	brush/brushes	bus/buses glass/glasses

RULES FOR ADDING –ed

Rules	Just add –ed*	When words end in e, drop e and add –ed	When words end in consonant + y, change the y to i and add –ed	When words end in vowel + y, just add –ed	If words end in 1 vowel + 1 consonant AND it is 1 syllable or stress is on last syllable, double the consonant	If words end in c, add a k before –ed
Words/ Examples	rent/rented wish/wished whisper/ whispered	free/freed issue/issued whistle/ whistled dye/dyed tape/taped hope/hoped	marry/ married carry/carried hurry/hurried	enjoy/enjoyed convey/ conveyed play/played	hop/hopped regret/ regretted stop/stopped rip/ripped tap/tapped	panic/panicked picnic/picnicked frolic/frolicked mimic/mimicked

* –ed can be added to a noun to form an adjective (left-handed; she is resolved; he is frustrated . . .)

APPENDIX E   *Modified Texts for Quizzes and Tests*

Apostrophes

PART ONE

Correct the following sentences.

1. *(2 errors)* Her friends brother asked, "Where are you goin after school?"

2. *(2 errors)* The students know its the 15th of February and there prone to counting the days until vacation.

3. *(2 errors)* The students teachers reminded them to avert they're eyes during the quiz.

4. *(2 errors)* There kitten was adorable when it put its paw in Chantals cup of milk.

5. *(2 errors)* Kathleen followed her intuition when she decided she didnt want to go to her friends birthday party.

CHALLENGE SENTENCE—EXTRA CREDIT: *(6 errors)*

My friends mothers baby cries when its noisy, when it's bottle is empty, and when their eating there dinner.

PART TWO

Write a paragraph that includes at least one example of each of the following five grammar rules you've learned:

1. Singular possessive

2. Plural possessive

3. Contractions

4. Dropped letters

5. Possessive pronouns

Possible topics for your paragraph

- Your favorite movie/book/video game

- What you plan to do over break next week

- The new school start time or other persuasive topic

Homophones

PART ONE

Directions: Edit the following paragraphs by circling the incorrect words and writing the correct spelling above the word. The first one has been underlined and corrected as an example.

                          Women's

March is <u>Womens</u> History Month. We would like you all to try and read (0)

one or two books about girl's who have made a difference or books by women (1)

author's as a way to celebrate and learn something knew. As you know, (2)

women didnt get the right to vote until the nineteenth amendment was added (1)

to the Constitution in 1920. Before 1920, there were to women who didn't (1)

avert there eye's from that prejudice: Elizabeth Cady Stanton and Susan B. (2)

Anthony. They fought hard to allow women they're right to vote. Although (1)

women have made a lot of progress, our country is not doing it's best. We have (1)

never had a female president, but womens intuition tells us that will change (1)

soon.

    On another note, all of your teacher's are hoping that you'll think about (1)

homophones every time you put your pen to paper. We no teenager's are (2)

prone to writing to quickly, so we want you to always reread you're writing (2)

slowly to check for error's. Otherwise, all these rule's you've learned wont ever (3)

become habits. That would be ideal and we hope your ready for that. And (1)

don't forget: use the words of the week in your sentence's in the next part and (1)

get extra credit!

Plural Spelling

Directions: There are twenty errors that you need to fix. Circle each one and write the correct spelling above the word. The first one has been underlined and corrected as an example.

                              visitors
In the middle of May, <u>visitor's</u> from all around New York City will come to (0)

speak to East Side middle school students about they're careers. We teachers (1)

know that you may think that its too early for you too start thinking about what (2)

kind of job you will pursue in the future, but its a great idea for you to be exposed to the (1)

different opportunitys that you may have. We know that some of you want to (1)

have familys, right? Some girls may want to be wifes and have a few babys, (3)

and some boys want to grow up to be strong mans and lead powerful lifes, but (2)

you have to start thinking about what else is out there. (0)

    Some people simply choose a career based on how much money theyll (1)

make or how famous they will be. However, many people work in numerous (0)

fields doing fascinating activitys that youve never even heard of. People (2)

who love there jobs don't just do it for the money. Instead, they (1)

usually have a passion for their work and want to share that passion with other (0)

people. That passion may be about curing sick animal's, preparing delectable (2)

lunchs for the homeless, drawing and painting in art studioes, counseling (2)

people about their crisises, and, of course, even teaching childs. You don't need a (2)

cape or a flashy uniform to be great—as long as you care about your job, (0)

all of you could be heros! (1)

Double Negatives and Indefinite Pronouns

Directions: Edit the following paragraphs by circling the incorrect words and writing the correct spelling above the word. The first one has been underlined and changed as an example.

A New York Hospital is at the center of fervor this week after two women were (0)

$$\text{weren't}$$

implanted with the wrong embryos. They <u>wasn't</u> able to (0)

complete no pregnancies and had to have emergency operations to remove (1)

the embryoes. Everybody at the hospital be furious that the two doctors (2)

who are responsible for the implantes haven't received no punishment, (2)

while the president of the hospital has been suspended! Both of the (0)

doctors is happy they didn't get in no trouble. (2)

   The womans intuition told them they was pregnant after the implant, (2)

and they was very happy because they was never able to make no babies (3)

on there own. They didnt have no idea that such a mistake could happen. (3)

Both is living in anguish. Many friends cames to there house to pacify (3)

them because their lifes are now in shambles. (1)

   One nurse at the hospital said, "It don't make no sense that the (2)

people who performed the implant are still working here! No one know if (1)

they might do it again." Several agrees. They think if the doctors can't (1)

read no instructions, then they shouldn't have there jobs. (2)

Bibliography

Angelillo, J. 2002. *A Fresh Approach to Teaching Punctuation: Helping Young Writers Use Conventions with Precision and Purpose*. New York: Scholastic.

Attewell, P., D. Lavin, T. Domina, and T. Levey. 2006. "New Evidence on College Remediation." *Journal of Higher Education* 77(5): 886–924.

Atwell, N. 2002. *Lessons That Change Writers*. Portsmouth, NH: Heinemann.

Barth, R. 2001. *Learning by Heart*. San Francisco: Jossey-Bass.

Bourdieu, P. 1986. "The Forms of Capital." *Handbook of Theory and Research in the Sociology of Education*, ed. J. E. Richardson, 241–58. Westport, CT: Greenwood Press.

———. 1991. *Language and Symbolic Power*. Cambridge: Harvard University Press.

Calkins, L. 1994. *The Art of Teaching Writing*. Portsmouth, NH: Heinemann.

Chajet, L. 2006. But Is What We Give Them Enough? Exploring Urban Small School Graduates' Journeys Through College. Unpublished doctoral dissertation, The City University of New York.

Delpit, L. 1995. *Other People's Children: Cultural Conflict in the Classroom*. New York: The New Press.

Ehrenworth, M., and V. Vinton. 2004. *The Power of Grammar: Unconventional Approaches to Conventions of Language*. Portsmouth, NH: Heinemann.

Gee, J. P. 2001. "Reading as Situated Language: A Sociocognitive Perspective." *Journal of Adolescent & Adult Literacy* 44(8): 714.

Martorell, P., and I. McFarlin. 2007. Help or Hindrance? The Effects of College Remediation on Academic and Labor Market Outcomes. Unpublished Report. Retrieved March 13, 2008 from https://editorialexpress.com/cgi-bin/conference/download .cgi?db_name= NASM2007&paper_id=726.

Robb, L. 2004. *Nonfiction Writing: From the Inside Out.* New York: Scholastic.

Smitherman, G. 1986. *Talkin and Testifyin: The Language of Black America.* Detroit: Wayne State University Press.

———. 2000. *Talkin That Talk: Language, Culture, and Education in African America.* New York: Routledge.

Snowball, D., and F. Bolton. 1999. *Spelling K–8: Planning and Teaching.* Portland, ME: Stenhouse.

Sparks, D. 2002. "In Search of Heroes: Give Educators a Place on the Pedestal—Interview with Roland Barth" [Electronic version]. *Journal of Staff Development* 23(1): 1–8.

Wheeler, R. S., and R. Swords. 2006. *Code-Switching: Teaching Standard English in Urban Classrooms.* Urbana, IL: National Council of Teachers of English.

Wiggins, G., and J. McTighe. 2005. *Understanding by Design.* Glenville, IL: Prentice Hall.